What Is Documentation?

English Translation of the Classic French Text

Suzanne Briet

Translated and edited by

Ronald E. Day
Laurent Martinet
with Hermina G. B. Anghelescu

The Scarecrow Press, Inc.
Lanham, Maryland • Toronto • Oxford
2006

SCARECROW PRESS, INC.

Published in the United States of America
by Scarecrow Press, Inc.
A wholly owned subsidary of
The Rowman & Littlefield Publishing Group, Inc.
4501 Forbes Boulevard, Suite 200, Lanham, Maryland 20706
www.scarecrowpress.com

PO Box 317
Oxford
OX2 9RU, UK

British Library Cataloguing in Publication Information Available

Library of Congress Cataloging-in-Publication Data

Briet, Suzanne, 1894–1989.
  [Qu'est-ce que la documentation? English]
  What is documentation? : English translation of the classic French text / Suzanne Briet ;
translated and edited by Ronald E. Day, Laurent Martinet with Hermina G.B.
Anghelescu.
    p. cm.
  Includes bibliographical references.
  ISBN-13: 978-0-8108-5109-2 (pbk. : alk. paper)
  ISBN-10: 0-8108-5109-1
  1. Documentation. 2. Information science. I. Day, Ronald E., 1959– II. Martinet,
Laurent, 1969– III. Anghelescu, Hermina G. B. IV. Title.

Z1001.B84513 2006
025—dc22
                                                                    2005023628

Contents

Preface   v

Acknowledgments   xi

A Brief Biography of Suzanne Renée Briet   1
Michael K. Buckland

Suzanne Briet's *What Is Documentation?*   9
Translated and edited by Ronald E. Day and
Laurent Martinet with Hermina G. B. Anghelescu

"A Necessity of Our Time": Documentation as
"Cultural Technique" in *What Is Documentation?*   47
Ronald E. Day

Writings by Suzanne Renée Briet:
A Selective Bibliography   65
Compiled by Michael K. Buckland

About the Editors and Contributors   71

~

Preface

> The forms that documentary work assumes are as numerous as the needs
> from which they are born.
>
> —Suzanne Briet, *What Is Documentation?*

Suzanne Briet (1894–1989) was an important European Documentalist, constituting what we may term the second generation of European Documentation. If the first generation may be thought of in terms of the work of the
founder of European Documentation, Paul Otlet (1868–1944), then the second generation might be thought of in terms of the work of Suzanne Briet,
and in particular, her small but important book, *What Is Documentation?*
What Is Documentation? is a revolutionary book in the field of library studies,
and it goes beyond Otlet's emphasis on the book as the trope and cornerstone
for documentation. It offers a vision beyond that of libraries and books, see-
ing in documentation an unlimited horizon of physical forms and aesthetic
formats for documents and an unlimited horizon of techniques and technologies (and of "documentary agencies" employing these) in the service of
multitudes of particular cultures. In these regards, Briet's manifesto remains a
"necessity for our time."

European Documentation was an important, but largely forgotten, movement bridging librarianship and what would become information science in
the first half of the twentieth century. Though it was a professional movement,

in the work of Otlet and Briet it was situated within the pressing concerns of its day: internationalization, standardization, documentary overload, coordinating and encouraging scholarly communication, and not least of all world peace (in Otlet) and international development (in Briet). In each of their works, consideration of not only the social orders in which documentation takes place, but also the *cultural forms and conditions for agency* of documentation, plays a central role. In contrast to the collection ethos and tradition of European librarianship, particularly before the Second World War, European documentation stressed services to the users within the contexts of cultural and intellectual expression and of social development. In contrast to librarianship on both sides of the Atlantic, documentation encouraged and foresaw the use of new technologies and new media in the delivery and production of information and knowledge. It emphasized the multiple physical forms and formats of documents and the importance of interlinking those forms through intermediary representations. In both Otlet's and Briet's works there is not only the embracing of new technologies, but also the celebration of such, and the desire to see the merging of human techniques and technologies in larger harmonies. Allied with, but going beyond, American Documentation on the one hand, and beyond American special librarianship on the other, European Documentation saw the integration of *technology* and *technique* (both may be rendered by the French word *technique*) within social development and cultural forms as the way forward. For all these reasons, European Documentation remains quintessentially a *modernist* phenomenon, one whose importance continues to this day, as we are still concerned with problems of documentary internationalization, standardization, technological and documentary convergence, documentary overload, scholarly communication, and the integration of technology, culture, and society across the globe. All those who have worked on the present translation and accompanying materials in this book have felt that it is imperative that Suzanne Briet's small book—really, a professional and cultural manifesto—be made available to readers of English.

Briet's *What Is Documentation?* originally appeared in 1951 from a small professional press, ÉDIT (Éditions Documentaires Industrielles et Techniques), which was a publishing arm of the Union Française des Organismes de Documentation (UFOD), of which Briet was a founding member. Out of negotiations between the now defunct UFOD and the Conservatoire national des Arts et Métiers (CNAM) came Briet's educational institution for documentation, the Institut national des techniques de la documentation (INTD), which still exists today and is located in CNAM. Briet's book appeared in a small printing and it sometimes reads as if it had little proofreading. Further, the printing is rather rough at points, with the chart at the end of the first chapter, in particular, being difficult to read because of awkward typographical alignments.

The book begins with the problem of defining documentation, which Briet does, as she explains, with the help of linguists and philosophers. Here, in the first of the three chapters ("A Technique of Intellectual Work"), Briet develops her notions of the concept and profession of documentation. Briet views documentation as a "cultural technique" that addresses the needs of contemporary culture at large and, most importantly, the needs of individual cultures of scientific disciplines and scholarly production, for the rapid and efficient delivery of documents toward scientific (and scholarly) advancement. In this latter role, the documentalist is attuned to particular cultures of research and production and to "prospecting" at the edge of and beyond those cultures for the benefit of researchers. What is important are the social networks and cultural forms that construct the meaning and value of documents. Within these networks and forms the documentalist locates—"orients"—him- or herself, though also in relation to neighboring networks and forms and in attunement to the demands of culture as a whole at a given time. The second chapter, "A Distinct Profession," lays out the professional specificity of documentation, particularly in regard to the traditional European librarianship of Briet's day, and it specifies the particular technologies and educational requirements that are needed in order to produce documentalists. For Briet, documentation surpasses librarianship by its attention to multiple forms and formats for documents and by a widened array of techniques to handle these. Documentary forms are becoming increasingly fragmentary, in contrast to the previous historical dominance of the book, and they are becoming recombined through standardized intermediaries. What is also striking—and of special importance for us, today—in this chapter is Briet's statement at one point that documentary forms are increasingly taking the shape of "substitutes for lived experiences"—that is, representational forms that assume the illusion of lived experience itself (film, photographs, etc.—echoing, but extending, earlier commentary in the twentieth century by Walter Benjamin and many others) and that these are being increasingly coordinated by abstract, standardized techniques toward a "collectivization of knowledge and ideas." These two aspects of documentary technique have, as Briet notes, consequences not only for professionals, but also for society at large. The last chapter, "A Necessity for Our Time," sums up the first two chapters and expands on the importance of documentation to society and culture in terms of international cooperation, emphasizing the work of the United Nations and UNESCO as important leadership organizations in world development. For Briet, documentation follows in the "wake" of the United Nations vessel, bringing development across the globe.

Professional activities, for Briet, can only be viable given an understanding of social and cultural space—and "culture" must be understood not just in terms of the sociology of production within individual scientific and scholarly disciplines, but also in regard to larger cultural, social, and historical horizons within which these disciplines, as well as documentation, may find or imagine itself. What Briet identifies as the failures of librarianship (and which her work in founding the reference room at the Bibliothèque nationale worked against) lies in its professional negligence for proactive engagement with, and on behalf of, these different cultures. For Briet, documentation is not only "dynamic," but it is also a dynamism of "*prospection*" ("research," or literally as our translation has rendered it, "prospecting"). Documentation, as Briet puts it elsewhere, must be like the "dog on the hunt," sniffing out new knowledge within and at the boundaries of established networks, resources, and materials, especially in fast-moving fields of research. And in doing so, it not only acknowledges, but also fits with, the new "rhythms" of production made possible by technology, which Briet understands as efficient and expansive.

These and other theoretical observations regarding documentation's relation to culture make Briet's book of value not only to Library and Information Studies, but also to cultural studies, rhetoric, and science and technology studies. The rhetorical and theoretical brilliance that characterize Briet's book have, perhaps, never been replicated in library and information publications and have rarely been seen in professional texts of any type. Not again—until Actor Network Theory at the end of the twentieth century—would a social network account of technical production, and specifically, documentary production, be articulated. Briet's comprehension of the integration of technology and technique, of machines and culture, is something that we still strive to understand in both Library and Information Studies and in science and technology studies. In terms of education and scholarship, there remains a large gulf between prescriptive, professional education and the study of larger cultural concerns, traditionally engaged in the liberal arts. Briet, however, points to the necessity of understanding and taking measure of the cultural categories, the historical lineages, and the social forces that produce, support, and continue a profession. She demands that documentalists be proficient in two foreign languages, that they consider the position of their work within a cultural specialty and within culture and society as a whole, that their orientation and specialized vocabularies originate from the cultural specialization which they serve, and that they see documents as assuming varieties of physical forms and formats. Briet believes that documentalists have as part of their mandate exploring at, and beyond, the boundaries of their cultural specialization. In these assertions, she challenges the education of library and information professionals in her day and in our own.

Thus, Briet's book points in many directions: it advocates on behalf of European documentation against the traditional boundaries and foci of librarianship and the education of library professionals, it engages in cultural analysis and critique, and it marks and foresees the transition from the culture of the book to the culture of documents in multiple forms and formats. It appears to simply be a professional manifesto, but it is so much more, and it is worth repeated readings for its complexity and subtlety. It is not only an important book of the past, but it is also an important book for the present and the future.

Ronald E. Day

~

Acknowledgments

We would like to thank the following people and organizations without whom this book would not have been possible: Renée Lemaître and Danièle Degez for their advice about the translation, Françoise Lauters for her assistance with copyright, Robert Pagès for his kind welcome and recollections about Suzanne Briet, and Michael Buckland for the biographical and bibliographical sections of this book and for doing so much to introduce Briet to contemporary scholarship worldwide. We would like to thank Hermina G. B. Anghelescu for reading an early version of this translation and making attentive and learned corrections to it; her work was invaluable in this project. We would also like to thank Suzanne Briet's heirs, Monsieur Jean-Paul Etienne and Monsieur Pascal Etienne, who very generously gave us permission to publish this translation. And last, we would like to thank Scarecrow Press for being willing to publish Briet's long-forgotten work and for their very generous permission to post sections of the present book electronically for the benefit of scholars and others across the globe.

Ronald E. Day
Laurent Martinet

~

A Brief Biography
of Suzanne Renée Briet

Michael K. Buckland

Suzanne Briet was born in Paris on February 1, 1894, but grew up in the Ardennes region in northern France. When married, during the 1930s, she used her married name, Suzanne Dupuy (or Dupuy-Briet), but then she reverted to using the surname Briet. On at least one occasion she used Briet-Cartulat, adding her mother's maiden name.

Briet qualified as a secondary school teacher of English and history, but after teaching in Algeria, from 1917 to 1920, she became a librarian. Qualifying in 1924, she was one of the first three women appointed as professional librarians in the Bibliothèque nationale in Paris. The feminization of librarianship occurred later in France than in the United States, essentially between the two World Wars. Many new ideas were being introduced at that time, some influenced by North American practice and encouraged by the Paris Library School that operated, under American Library Association sponsorship, from 1923 to 1929. It must have been an exciting and interesting situation in spite of the political and economic difficulties and, later, the Second World War.

Briet's main professional achievement at the Bibliothèque nationale was symbolic of her interest in service and modernization: She planned, established, and supervised (from 1934 to 1954) the Salle des Catalogues et Bibliographies, which was created by remodeling a basement.[1] Here, bibliographies, which had previously been kept in closed stacks, were made available.

She organized supplementary indexing and developed a bibliographic advisory service. The cross of the Legion of Honor was conferred on her in this room in 1950.

From the late 1920s onwards, Briet was active nationally and internationally in the development of what was then called Documentation but would now be called Information Management or Information Science. She participated in the founding (in 1931) and in the subsequent leadership of the Union Française des Organismes de Documentation (UFOD), the French analogue of the American Documentation Institute (founded in 1937 and now called the American Society for Information Science and Technology). She was a leader in developing professional education for this new specialty. She developed (and UFOD adopted) a plan for what would have been the first school of Documentation / Information Science worldwide, had it been established at that time. When, in 1951, such a school was established, the Institut national des techniques de la documentation at the Conservatoire national des Arts et Métiers, Briet was the founding Director of Studies.[2] She became vice president of the International Federation for Documentation (FID) and acquired the nickname "Madame Documentation."

Briet's remarkable manifesto on the nature of documentation, *Qu'est-ce que la documentation?* ("What Is Documentation?") (Paris: EDIT, 1951) is a pamphlet of 48 pages. Part I seeks to push the boundaries of the field beyond texts to include any material form of evidence ("Is a living animal a document?" Briet asks). Part II argues that a new and distinct profession was emerging. Part III urges the societal need for new and active documentary services. This tract may seem at first to be enthusiastic hyperbole, but it remains significant because it is still relevant to understanding the nature, scope, and societal impacts of documents and documentation.[3] Briet's modernist perspective, combined with semiotics, deserves attention now because it is different from, and offers an alternative to, the scientific, positivist view that has so dominated information science and which is increasingly questioned. A Spanish edition appeared in 1960,[4] but it has not appeared in English until now. Until recently, it has hardly been mentioned in the English-language literature. Verner Clapp wrote a perceptive review.[5]

In 1954, at the age of 60, Briet took early retirement. She left librarianship and documentation and concentrated on other interests. For another thirty years she wrote about the history of the Ardennes region in northern France, her ancestral homeland, and of individuals born there, including the brilliant young poet Arthur Rimbaud whom she viewed as an enduring symbol of the human spirit.[6] She wrote a sympathetic biography of Rimbaud's tough mother,[7] a life of Jean, Comte de Montdejeux (a seventeenth-century warrior),[8] some poetry, and much more. She died in 1989 in Paris at age 95, largely forgotten in her professional field until a renewed interest in her ideas emerged during the 1990s.

Briet's historical and literary studies are carefully documented. Her *What Is Documentation?* in contrast, is a manifesto. Persuasion is expected to follow from the arguments and facts presented, not from sources cited, nor from the authority of the author. Thus a pivotal statement defining "document" as a form of evidence is attributed to a "contemporary bibliographer concerned about clarity" who is not identified. A quotation about how facts become "clothed" in texts is attributed to her friend, the philosopher Raymond Bayer, but no citation is given. Briet writes with confidence, but, otherwise, there is little indication of what qualifications she brings. In fact, however, Briet generated some hundred publications in the 60 years from 1925 to 1985 that reveal a wide range of interests and activities, but even knowing that does not adequately reveal how very well qualified she was to explain documentation. (See the selected bibliography included in this volume.)

First, Briet had been deeply engaged in the documentation movement from the late 1920s onward, serving on committees, developing professional education, participating in conferences, and serving as vice president of the International Federation for Documentation and as secretary-general of the French association for documentation, UFOD.

Second, Briet had a deep grounding in culture and in the humanities. She studied English and history and she published literary studies and contributions to the regional history of the Ardennes. More relevant to her manifesto, she understood that technology and culture were deeply connected. She saw society and, therefore, culture, as being reshaped by technology. The techniques of documentation in aiding and shaping intellectual work were, in her view, both a symptom of, and a contributory force within, the "industrialization" of knowledge workers. We can now see, with the impact of computers and telecommunications, how right she was.

Third, like other librarians at the Bibliothèque nationale, Briet was well connected in the intellectual world and, probably, more so than most because of her role in the Salle des Catalogues, essentially a major reference library.

Fourth, like other leading figures in documentation, Briet was acutely aware of the importance of standards, collaboration, and interoperability. She helped to coordinate the development of library-related standards in France after the Second World War. She was partly responsible for the development of a French cataloging code and her Salle des Catalogues served as secretariat for that effort. Internationally she served on the International Standards Organization T46 Committee, which was responsible for standards in relation to Documentation. An overview of standards development in France in the postwar years commented in glowing terms on Briet's "remarkable erudition" and "inexhaustible patience."[9]

Fifth, Briet understood how organizations worked. She was employed in the Bibliothèque nationale, a complex government agency; she founded a successful Rotary club for women; and she was elected president of the Union of European Women and honorary president of the Amis de Rimbaud, in addition to her leadership roles in FID and UFOD.

Finally, she was an accomplished and experienced professional: as a librarian, as an educator, as a scholar, and in related tasks. She curated a major exhibition, with more than a thousand exhibits and a detailed, annotated catalog, to mark the centenary of Rimbaud's birth.[10]

Briet was, in these ways, unusually well qualified to ask and to answer the question *What Is Documentation?* In addition, a level of practical wisdom is reflected in her views of the relationship between librarianship and documentation, which seem to have been reinforced by her tour of the United States in 1951–1952, examining bibliographic services, reference service, and professional education. She concluded that the Americans had a high level of achievement in "documentation" even though few of them were familiar with that term. She recognized that, because of the vigor of the special libraries movement in the United States, what might have been called a documentation center in France would generally have been regarded as a special library in the United States. This insight makes her trip reports interestingly different from the usual practice of making forced distinctions between documentation and librarianship.[11]

In 1954 Briet wrote a noteworthy paper on the relationship between librarianship and documentation.[12] In her view, librarians and documentalists are not different in kind but, rather, in their emphasis: Librarians tend collections and develop bibliographic apparatus; documentalists focus on advancing the intellectual work of the groups they serve. Differences in type of material selected, forms of indexing, and timeliness flow from that difference in emphasis. Reference librarians and special librarians occupy an intermediate position. There is a tinge of exasperation at the number of people who, instead, wanted to insist on unification or rigid partition. Written in the year she retired from the field, this paper can be seen as a professional swan song. If more people had adopted Briet's enlightened views the disruptive antagonisms between "traditional librarians" and "information science" in the ensuing decades might have been avoided.

Her memoirs, *Entre Aisne et Meuse . . . et au delà* ("Between the Aisne and the Meuse . . . and beyond"),[13] are similarly understated. She provides a collection of wry, whimsical, and nostalgic anecdotes and observations arranged, appropriately for a documentalist, under keywords in alphabetical order. For 25 years she had been in the forefront with the pioneers who were then the leaders in the field: Samuel Bradford, Watson Davis, Jean Gérard, Paul Otlet, Walter Schürmeyer, Jean Wyart, and others. Her memory and insights would have been a wonderful source for us to understand better that important, but neglected period, but there is no mention of any of those people and very little of that part of her life in her memoirs. Once again, one wants more, but, for Briet, it may have seemed boastful and in poor taste to have described her own achievements, and improper and indiscrete to have commented on those of her colleagues.

Acknowledgments

I am grateful for help received from Samia Benidir, Michael Carpenter, J. Periam Danton, Ronald E. Day, and Mary Niles Maack.

This paper expands Michael Buckland, "The Centenary of 'Madame Documentation': Suzanne Briet, 1894–1989," *Journal of the American Society for Information Science* 46, no. 3 (April 1995): 235–37, also published in French as "Le centenaire de `Madame Documentation': Suzanne Briet, 1894–1989," *Documentaliste: Sciences de l'information* 32, no. 3 (mai/juin 1995): 179–81, and summarized as "Suzanne Briet, 1894–1989," in *Dictionnaire encyclopédique de l'information et de la documentation*, ed. Serge Cacaly. Collection REF. (Paris: Éditions Nathan, 1997), 105–6.

The biographical details are based on the lengthy obituary of Briet by Renée Lemaître and Paul Roux-Fouillet, "Suzanne Briet (1894–1989)," *Bulletin d'Informations de l'Association des bibliothécaires français*, 144 (1989): 55–56. (1989), and also on:

Bruno Delmas, "L'INTD et son rôle dans la formation des documentalistes en France 1932–1993," *Documentaliste* 30 (1993): 218–26.
"Contributions à l'histoire de la Documentation en France," Special issue, *Documentaliste* 30, no. 4/5 (juillet–octobre 1993): 189–284.
Sylvie Fayet-Scribe, *Histoire de la documentation en France: Culture, science et technologie de l'information 1895–1937* (Paris: CNRS, 2000).
"Hommage à Madame Suzanne Briet," *Rimbaud vivant. Bulletin des Amis de Rimbaud* 26 (1987): 1–13. Includes portrait; Jean Guirec, "Suzanne Briet"; Pierre Petitfils, "Notre Présidente d'Honneur" [Briet biobibliography]; and a poem by S. Briet.
Mary Niles Maack, "Women Librarians in France: The First Generation," *Journal of Library History* 18 (1983): 407–49.

―――, "The Lady and the Antelope: Suzanne Briet's Contribution to the French Documentation Movement," *Library Trends* 52, no. 4 (Spring 2004): 719–47.

Pamela Spence Richards, "Scientific Information in Occupied France, 1940–44," *Library Quarterly* 62 (1992): 295–305.

Notes

1. Julien Cain, *Les transformations de la Bibliothèque nationale et le Dépôt annexe de Versailles* (Paris: Editions des Bibliothèques nationales, 1936), 33–34; Suzanne Briet, "Bibliography in the Basement," *Special Libraries* 41 (1950): 52–55.

2. "Les cours techniques de documentation," *Journal of Documentation* 1, no. 2 (Sept. 1945): 89–92; Bruno Delmas, "Une fonction nouvelle: Genèse et développement des centres de documentation," in *Histoire des bibliothèques françaises*, vol. 4, *Les bibliothèques au XXe siècles, 1914–1990* (Paris: Promodis—Editions du cercle de la librairie, 1992), 178–93.

3. Michael Buckland, "Information as Thing," *Journal of the American Society of Information Science* 42, no. 5 (June 1991): 351–60, or at www.sims.berkeley.edu/~buckland/thing.html (accessed March 26, 2005); Michael Buckland, "What is a 'Document'?" *Journal of the American Society for Information Science* 48, no. 9 (Sept 1997): 804–9, or at www.sims.berkeley.edu/~buckland/whatdoc.html (accessed March 26, 2005); Ronald E. Day, *The Modern Invention of Information: Discourse, History, and Power* (Carbondale: Southern Illinois University Press, 2001).

4. Suzanne Briet, *Que es la documentación?* trans. Beatriz Favaro (Argentina, Santa Fé: Universidad nacional del Litoral. Facultad de ciencias jurídicas y sociales. Departamento del extensión universitaria, 1960).

5. Verner Clapp, [Review of *Qu'est-ce que la documentation?*] Library of Congress Information Bulletin 11 (1952): 1–3.

6. Suzanne Briet, *Rimbaud notre prochain* (Paris: Nouvelle éditions latines, 1956).

7. Suzanne Briet, *Madame Rimbaud, essai de biographie, suivi de la correspondance de Vitalie Rimbaud-Cuif dont treize lettres inédites Avant-siècle 5* (Paris: Lettres modernes, Minard, 1968).

8. Suzanne Briet, *Le Maréchal de Schulemberg: Jean III, comte de Montdejeux (1598–1671).* (Les cahiers d'études ardennais 4). (Mézières: Editions de la Société d'Études Ardennaises, Archives départementales, 1960).

9. J. Birlé, "Quelques aspects de la normalisation française dans le domaine de la documentation," in International Federation for Documentation, 17th Conference, Berne, 1947. *Rapports* (The Hague: F.I.D., 1947) 1: 103–7.

10. Bibliothèque Nationale, *Arthur Rimbaud. Exposition organisée pour le centième anniversaire de sa naissance* (Paris: Bibliothèque nationale, 1954).

11. Suzanne Briet, "Bibliothèques et centres de documentation technique aux États Unis: Notes d'un voyage de quatre mois (Octobre 1951–Février 1952)," *ABCD:*

Archives, Bibliothèques, Collections, Documentation 11 (1952): 299–308; Suzanne Briet, "La formation professionnelle des bibliothécaires aux États-Unis," *ABCD: Archives, Bibliothèques, Collections, Documentation* 13 (1954): 337–40; "Madame Suzanne Briet," *Library of Congress Information Bulletin* 10, no. 45 (1951): 9; Suzanne Briet, *Entre Aisne et Meuse . . . et au delà*, Les cahiers ardennais 22 (Charleville-Mezières: Société des Ecrivains Ardennais, 1976), 34–36.

12. Suzanne Briet, "Bibliothécaires et documentalistes" *Revue de la Documentation* 21, fasc. 2 (1954): 41–45.

13. Briet, *Entre Aisne et Meuse . . . et au delà*, 34–36.

~

Suzanne Briet's
What Is Documentation?

Translated and edited by Ronald E. Day and Laurent
Martinet with Hermina G. B. Anghelescu

1951
Édit
Éditions Documentaires
Industrielles et Techniques
17 Rue de Grenelle, Paris (7è)

Collection of Documentology

I. A Technique of Intellectual Work
II. A Distinct Profession
III. A Necessity of Our Time

I. A Technique of Intellectual Work

For Julien CAIN[1]

From the very beginning, Latin culture and its heritage have given to the word *document* the meaning of instruction or proof. RICHELET's dictionary, just as LITTRÉ's, are two French sources that bear witness to this. A contemporary bibliographer concerned about clarity has put forth this brief definition: "A document is a proof in support of a fact."

If one refers to the "official" definitions of the French Union of Documentation Organizations [l'Union Française des Organismes de Documentation], one ascertains that the document is defined as "all bases of materially fixed knowledge, and capable of being used for consultation, study, and proof."

This definition has often been countered by linguists and philosophers, who are, as they should be, infatuated with minutia and logic. Thanks to their analysis of the content of this idea, one can propose here a definition, which may be, at the present time, the most accurate, but is also the most abstract, and thus, the least accessible: "any concrete or symbolic indexical sign [*indice*], preserved or recorded toward the ends of representing, of reconstituting, or of proving a physical or intellectual phenomenon."

Is a star a document? Is a pebble rolled by a torrent a document? Is a living animal a document? No. But the photographs and the catalogues of stars, the stones in a museum of mineralogy, and the animals that are cataloged and shown in a zoo, are documents.

In our age of multiple and accelerated broadcasts, the least event, scientific or political, once it has been brought into public knowledge, immediately becomes weighted down under a "vestment of documents" [*vêture de documents*] (Raymond Bayer[2]). Let us admire the documentary fertility of a simple originary fact: for example, an antelope of a new kind has been encountered in Africa by an explorer who has succeeded in capturing an individual that is then brought back to Europe for our Botanical Garden [Jardin des Plantes]. A press release makes the event known by newspaper, by radio, and by newsreels. The discovery becomes the topic of an announcement at the Academy of Sciences. A professor of the Museum discusses it in his courses. The living animal is placed in a cage and cataloged (zoological garden). Once it is dead, it will be stuffed and preserved (in the Museum). It is loaned to an Exposition. It is played on a soundtrack at the cinema. Its voice is recorded on a disk. The first monograph serves to establish part of a treatise with plates, then a special encyclopedia (zoological), then a general encyclopedia. The works are cataloged in a library, after having been announced at publication (publisher catalogues and Bibliography of France[3]). The documents are recopied (drawings, watercolors, paintings, statues, photos, films, microfilms), then selected, analyzed, described, translated (documentary productions). The documents that relate to this event are the object of a scientific classifying (fauna) and of an ideologic [*idéologique*] classifying (classification). Their ultimate conservation and utilization are determined by some general techniques and by methods that apply to all documents—methods that are studied in national associations and at international Congresses.

The cataloged antelope is an initial document and the other documents are secondary or derived.

GUTENBERG's invention has created such a voluminous and intense typographical production, especially in the last one hundred years, that the problem of the conservation and utilization of graphic documents[4] became acute. Since the seventeenth century, the abundance of written documents has required a scientific method of prospecting [*prospection*] and of classifying books and manuscripts—*bibliography*. Louise-Noelle MALCLÈS[5] has defined "bibliography" thus: "Bibliography is the knowledge of all published or copied texts. It is based on the research, the identification, the description, and the classification of documents, in view of organizing services or building instruments that are aimed toward facilitating intellectual work. One particular technique unites these different steps...the four successive operations constitute the technique, or the science, of bibliography, and they result in catalogues that are themselves called bibliographies. . . . It appears necessary, then, to separate two senses of the word and to distinguish a bibliographical theory which establishes rules of research and of classification, and a bibliographical practice which applies such rules to the production of tools of research, which are themselves bibliographies."

The central reserves which constitute the great national libraries (Paris, 7 million imprints, Washington, 8,700,000) could not dominate—or, we would gladly say, tame—their riches and place them at the disposal of a wider and wider public without the help of tools which allow access to the documents which are collected there. Current *catalogues*, retrospective catalogues, and union catalogues are obligatory documentary tools, and they are the practical intermediaries between graphical documents and their users. These catalogues of documents are themselves documents of a secondary degree.

With the specialization of studies and the multiplication of all kinds of activities that we see proliferating throughout our society, relations and points of view have taken on greater mobility and more variety (BLISS[6]). "Knowledge and studies, science and practice could not exist without the efficient exploration of documents and a rigorous organization of documentary work."

Out of such a need appear *centers and departments of documentation*, which are the most dynamic agencies of documentation. Directories of documentary agencies have appeared in many countries. (France 1935, 1942, 1948, 1951; Great Britain 1928; the Netherlands 1937; Belgium 1947; Switzerland 1946).

Thus, a new profession is born—*that of the documentalist*—that corresponds to the functions of the person who documents others. The documentalist is that person who performs the craft of documentation. He must possess the techniques, methods, and tools of documentation. It is now possible for this person to become a licensed technician: a state diploma exists in France since the establishment of the National Institute of Documentary Techniques [Institut National des Techniques de la Documentation (INTD)], attached to the National Conservatory of Arts and Crafts [Conservatoire National des Arts et Métiers], (Decree of December the first, 1950).

Little by little, the theory of documentation has grown since the great period of the typographical explosion that began in the third quarter of the nineteenth century, which corresponds to the development of the historical sciences as the progress of technique. OTLET had been its magus, the international leader, with his Institute of Bibliography in Brussels, his universal decimal classification system, his Council of Scientific Unions, and his Mundaneum. Others, less ambitious—or, more prudent—plowed the furrows of a culture that failed, in Otlet's circle, to descend from the clouds. *Documentology*[7] lost nothing in alleviating itself of a Universal Bibliographic Catalog [Répertoire Bibliographique Universel—RBU], which everyone had considered a dream and which did not offer a comparable attraction to the most localized of union catalogues.

While the book, originally issuing from the leaf, presently tends to burst in its constitutive elements because of the need for mobility, other documentary forms appear through modern inventions and enrich the collection of human tools thanks to documentographies.[8] One is no longer content with the book, with the printed fragment, the review article, the newspaper clipping, the archival copy. One transfers an entire work with its illustrations onto microfilms, microfiches, and onto "microcards." A thick binder, microfilmed, can fit into a vest pocket. An entire library is contained in a handbag. The scientific quest extends itself to documentary items of all types, iconographic, metallic, monumental, megalithic, photographic, radio-televised. The selection of documents annexes to itself the newest techniques. "Pre-documentalist" professions, themselves, set off along this race toward documents. The young generations of archivists and museum specialists decipher ancient texts with the microfilm "reader" and create photo-fiches where the image of the museum piece sits next to its scientific description, as at the Documentation Center for Egyptology and at the Carnavalet Museum. The most venerable libraries annex to themselves offices of documentation and photographic laboratories, such as the Bibliothèque Nationale in Paris, which shows its productivity in the areas of microfilm and color photography. Enormous collections of films and photographs are amassed in Washington at the Library of Congress and at the State Archives.

Documentary unity tends to get close to the elementary idea, to the unity of thought, while the forms of documents grow, the amount of documents increase, and the techniques of the documentalist craft are perfected.

Documentation for oneself or for others has appeared in the eyes of many people as *"a cultural technique"* of a new type.

This technique has prospered, first of all, in the area of scientific research, properly speaking, that is, in the sciences and their applications. The human sciences adopted it more belatedly. One can easily understand the reasons for this. Indeed, in the fields of science and technology [*technique*], documentation is almost constantly renewed, in a very narrow time span; this or that invention or discovery have become outmoded facts, and thus, too well known to be used as the object of new studies. In contrast, in the fields of the human sciences, documentation proceeds by accumulation: literature, history, philosophy, law, economics, and the history of the sciences itself are tributaries of the past. Erudition is conservative. Science is revolutionary. *The evolution of human knowledge* is a permanent compromise between two mental attitudes. Invention and explanation, reflection and hypothesis divide the field of thought. Documentation is their servant: blithe as a milkmaid,[9] or sumptuously dressed according to the wishes of its masters, the scholars.

The *evolution of intellectual work* manifests itself on the scholar's worktable. The conditions and the tools of mental work today are very different from what they previously were. MONTAIGNE retired in his round tower, BOSSUET to the bishop's garden, DESCARTES in his secret dwelling, EDISON locked himself away. Spinoza only had sixty books. In Louis XIV's France, only seventy books a year were published. Now there appears an average of 12,000, not counting reprints. In 1947, five million volumes had been published in the United States, of which 40 percent were textbooks. Seven million diverse documents come in each year to the Library of Congress in Washington. Important centers of documentation receive and regularly abstract between 100 and 2,000 journals. The entries in the Bulletin de Documentation Bibliographique, the current French bibliography of bibliographies, amount to about 2,000 to 2,500 per year.

800,000 periodical articles had appeared before the last world war. The Periodical Department[10] handles more than a million French and foreign items a year, some of which duplicate those in the French legal deposit.

French Legal Deposit	1939	1948	1950
French national works	9,908	14,143	9,943
Translations	851	1,088	1,009
Non-French publications	1,767	789	797
	12,526	16,020	11,849

BRADFORD has shown that the analyses of scientific articles find themselves redone in several periodicals, most often two or three times, while missing from the important proportion of half of the periodicals. The same BRADFORD (thanks to some statistical surveys which allowed him to formulate the so-called "Bradford's law") has had the merit of specifying the percentage (33%) of noteworthy articles on a particular subject that could be found in journals specializing in another subject. Moreover, a detailed study of the work of analytical journals led him to the conclusion that, in principle, two-thirds of the collections of specialized documentation agencies did not directly relate to the profile of the agency, and that nonetheless, the totality of the documentation of interest to the specialty couldn't be found anywhere.

The cumulative documentation at the disposal of the human sciences overwhelms in importance and in quantity the figures, however impressive, of scientific production, per se. It seems that an Ariadne's thread may be still more important to a humanist than to a scientist.[11] The immense libraries with which the scholar surrounds himself, and those which he consults beyond his abode, are for him a field of exploration, partly untapped. The systematic use of witnesses of the past is not possible. The investigation, here, is in a freer manner than in the scientific domains. "The margin for personal choice" is larger (PAGÈS[12]).

Still, the tools of intellectual work have deeply transformed the attitude of the scholar, whatever his specialty may be. The factors of space and time intervene much more than in the past. The hourly calendar, the telephone, the microfilm reader, the typewriter, the Dictaphone, and the teletype give to intellectual work a *different rhythm*.

"At the beginning of knowledge there is the examination of facts," said BACON. CARNEGIE[13] advised to never undertake an enterprise "before having thoroughly examined all the works" which may have already been done on the subject in question. The problem may be, rather, of selecting the best works. It is upon this problem that a competency is necessary. It is there that a rigorous method comes to the rescue of the researcher. "Order is the rarest of things in the operations of the mind" said FÉNELON. Order, marking, selection: three essential steps in intellectual occupations.

In the task of "collectivizing" knowledge, which is truly of our time, the *documentary analysis* or "abstract"[14] has appeared as one of the most rapid and most reliable means of announcing and communicating thought. It is the role of specialized libraries, of centers of documentation, and of technical journals to put on the desk of the specialist an analytical and sometimes critical resume of new things that interest him, and which permit him to detect the sources that he can, if he so desires, utilize by way of reading the material directly or by way of photographic reproduction. Data processing responds to the needs of a research that works upon masses of documents with easily codified statistical indices.

At the forefront of scientific and technical research, modern documentation has become one of the most effective factors of *productivity* throughout all areas. It will suffice to take two examples: that of the CNRS[15] and that of NEYRPIC.[16] The National Center of Scientific Research [CNRS], with its teams of abstractors and specialized translators, with its journal collections and its microfilm service, has established itself in the minds of our scholars as an institution that one would not know how to do without. The NEYRET-PICTET firm, with its documentation service very strongly related to the activities of the laboratories, of the shops and of the research units, made immense progress in the application of hydraulics throughout the world.

Orientation guides have made known those possibilities that are available through conservators and distributors of documentation or information. They have been nationally established for all scientific interests and activities, or for a group that is more or less widespread throughout a country. Manuals of Documentary Research have been created in France to point the researcher to the best works, periodical article, centers and associations, libraries and museums, and specialized publishers.

Scientific research has become aware of itself in nearly all fields. In order to leave behind "chaos" and documentary bottleneck, collective undertakings of research and documentation were organized. The documentalist has become a "team player" (VERNE[17]). He has played his role in solving the problem that consists in "giving free rein" to the "individual and subconscious investigating capabilities of each, while placing at the disposal of all the documentation which interests a group of researchers" (WIGNER[18]). The documentalist freed the individual labor of the scientist from ponderous servitude. Under any circumstances, this requires that the documentalist know the specialty that he professionally assists and it requires that he gather the bibliography, or better, the documentography accumulated by the researchers themselves. Files on the competencies, interests, and gaps of the researchers may be of the greatest interest (documentation on persons and possibilities for collective research).

Documentation, while it is intimately tied to the life of a team of workers or scientists or scholars—or while it participates in an industrial, commercial, administrative, teaching activity, etc., can in certain cases end in a genuine *creation*, through the juxtaposition, selection, and the comparison of documents, and the production of auxiliary documents. The content of documentation is, thus, inter-documentary.

There are other problems of documentation that scholars lately have underlined with a certain vehemence. Namely, in regard to the speed of service and to the completeness of documentary information. The American professor, BURCHARD,[19] while recognizing the dynamism and efficiency of librarians in his country, reckons that science found its Waterloo in libraries. According to him, interlibrary loan is a process of delayed action. The union catalogue entails a long waiting period. For several years, even if one is in a better position to rapidly obtain a photo or microfilm, the *time factor* still remains no less formidable for the time-pressed scholar. The ephemeral nature of scientific information imposes upon the worker in this area a certain intellectual behavior and it demands adequate tools. As ever, the scholar obtains information by his personal relations, by his readings, and by the bibliography that he finds there. But more and more, he becomes informed by abstracts[20] and by reports. Microfilm brings to the scientific researcher in his laboratory, onto his writing table, the document itself, as a small volume and in its entirety.

Is the scholar confident of having the power to locate *the entirety of that documentation* which interests him? The centers and offices of documentation read it for him. Documentary work is organized collectively. However, an important part of scientific documentation remains secret, in certain areas at least. Jean THIBAUD[21] has recently translated [*a traduit*] the anxiety of scholars regarding the fact that "science" now appears "as the most essential of warlike activities in a time of peace." The great EINSTEIN has given the cry of alarm: "the field of information unceasingly shrinks under the pressure of military necessity." Secret documentation is an insult inflicted upon documentation.

The moment has arrived to prove that the exercise of documentation, with all its possibilities and all its perfected means, effectively constitutes a *new cultural technique*. Documentation is becoming more and more technical, as a specialized skill. M. Le ROLLAND[22] has told us that the hand provides for thought, just as a task which is partly manual serves culture, that is to say, it enriches man. He cites Julian HUXLEY[23]: "The hands receive a precise tactile image from the materials they handle, the eyes receive a precise image from what they see. . . . The most complete definition of objects by conceptual thought has been followed by their most complete mastery by means of tools and machines." The hand has served the mind; the tool has developed the brain. The brain in turn guides the hand. Such is the omnipresence of intelligence. "Documentation is to culture as the machine is to industry" (PAGÈS).

It is not too much to speak of a new *humanism* in this regard. A different breed of researchers "is in the making."[24] It springs from the reconciliation of the machine and the mind. Modern man cannot repudiate any aspect of his heritage. Relying on the rich experiences of the past that have been passed on to him, he resolutely turns toward the world of tomorrow. The constant development of humanity requires that the masses and the individual adapt. Here, technology [*technique*] is the symptom of a social need. "One characteristic of modern documentation is that of the coordination" of diverse "sectors in the same organization."

Thus, documentation appears as the *corrective* to ever advancing *specialization*. Closed within the more or less spacious limits of his specialty, the researcher needs to be guided through the frontier regions of his particular domain. Orientation along the margins of a subject, prospecting some of the sources in an area of research, determining expertise—these are the many requirements involved in the coordination of diverse activities.

[*Translators' Note:* In the original printing of the following chart, the alignment of terms between columns is not exact. The following constitutes our best reading of Briet's chart.]

	"docere"[1]	DOCUMENTATION	
		Makes known:	
			ORGANIZATIONS
OBJECT	ACTIVITIES	FORMS	[ORGANISMES]
1st degree (Instruction) a. Facts or ideas	by means of: *Information* verbal: written:	Pieces of Information. Communiqués journals, and reviews.	A, L, M.* Firms of documentation. Post–Press.
	cinema-radio:	Films.	Cinema–Radio.
	Teaching verbal: written:	Pulpits. Lectures. Laboratories. Catalogs–guides.	Churches. Schools and Universities. Associations. Research.
b. Objects or artistic creation	*Exhibition* direct or reproduced	Objects. Specimens. Animals. Photos.	Congresses–Fairs. *Exhibition* Committees. A, L, M.
	Performances live or recorded	Catalogs–Programs Disks. Cards.	Concerts. Theaters.
c. Persons or activities	*Information* [*Renseignements*]:	Dossiers. Registers. Announcements. Year-books and directories.	Police– Statistics Registry offices Associations– Societies.
d. Sources of facts	*Inventories:* Commerical or official editions	Dictionaries and grammars. Chronologies. Atlases and guides. Treatises and manuals. Legal, legislative, historical and literary texts. Encyclopedias. Patents. Catalogs.	A, L, M. Authors and Publishers. Academies. Learned Societies STATE PATENT OFFCE
	Consultation or *Communication* and organized reading.		A, L, M.

INSTRUCTION

PROSPECTION

DIFFUSION

ORGANIZATION

OBJECT	ACTIVITIES	FORMS	ORGANIZATIONS [ORGANISMES]
2nd degree (Exploration) [Prospection] Sources of documents	by means of: *bibliographic orientation:*	Card Files. Registers. *Catalogs.* Bibliographies and documentographies. Research guides. Lists of sources. Lists of organizations.	Archives. Libraries. Museums. CENTERS OF DOCUMENTATION.
3rd degree (Diffusion) Collectively used or individually adapted documents	by means of: *Documentary production* by selection, analysis, translation, reproduction, grouping, distribution	Selections. Extracts. Analyses. Reports. Translations. Dossiers. Photos. Documentary editions. [*Editions doc.*]	Archives. Libraries. Museums. CENTERS OF DOCUMENTATION.
4th degree (Organization) Documentology	by means of: *Cooperation,* Standardization [*Normalization*] and *Documentary orientation*	Lectures. Bulletins. Manuals. Commissions. Courses.	A Congress. L Associations. M Committees. AFNor[2] /ISO UFOD[3] /FID[4] / UNESCO. Schools of documentation Centers of documentology

*A, L, M: Archives, Libraries, and Museums
[1]"Docere": Latin verb meaning to teach something to someone; to bring someone to a state of knowledge.
[2]AFNor (Association Française de Normalization): French Association of Standardization.
[3]UFOD (Union Française des Organismes de Documentation): French Union of Documentation Organizations.
[4]FID (Fédération Internationale de Documentation): International Federation for Documentation.

II. A Distinct Profession

For Louis RAGEY[25]

"Homo documentator" is born out of new conditions of research and technology [*technique*].

While in certain countries, such as Great Britain, the archival trade is treated with good reason as a "new profession," modern archives are more and more closely similar to, properly speaking, centers of documentation, as RAGANATHAN has not failed to point out. Most administrative papers are distributed in the form of type or print. Most official publications take a periodical form. The file, the memorandum, the report are treated as documentary elements, and not as library books. Libraries, deprived of the more mobile forms of documentation (printed, typed, photographed, etc.) remain the distributors of documentation of the past, but they see research at all its stages escape from them, retaining only the exhibition of acquired facts. Major instruments in the preservation and conservation of culture, general libraries follow with inevitable slowness the progress of knowledge and the progress of the technical approach to documents. Specialized libraries are much closer to the centers of research, and for the most part they tend to transform into centers of documentation, with or without the name. The "information" or "intelligence officers,"[26] that one has seen multiply in the industrial centers of Great Britain or the United States, are the first cousins of French "documentalists." Trained or not in library schools, they are born out of the same specialized cultural environment as the institution of which they are part. They satisfy all the requirements of the creed by which the *documentalist* is: first, a subject specialist, that is to say, that he possesses a cultural specialization related to that of the institution where he is employed; second, understands the techniques of the form of documents and their treatment (choice, conservation, selection, reproduction); third, respects the documents in their physical and intellectual integrity; fourth, is capable of proceeding to an interpretation and selection of the value of the documents which he is responsible for in view of their distribution or documentary synthesis.

Robert PAGÈS has put forward that the professions of the librarian, archivist, and museum curator were "pre-documentalist" professions and, that the librarian was becoming in our time "a particular kind of documentalist." This is absolutely not about precedence. Graphic documentation being much more voluminous in the present as in the past, the traditional techniques of preservation and of the history of book collections and assimilated documents will maintain for a long time still a preeminence that is beyond dispute. But already for the great collections of the past the word "bibliography" is no longer appropriate, even if one could give it a meaning large enough to cover catalogs of all types. For the presence in a library of busts, medals, geographical maps, and personal memorabilia demand that one henceforth use the word "documentography."

It is not rare that the documentalist is found at the head of an establishment that contains a specialized library, a research section, an analytical and/or bibliographical newsletter, a photo-microfilm service, an exhibition hall, press clippings, and translations. Archivist, librarian, collection curator —our documentalist is all these at once. He thus needs—beside his initial cultural specialization—to be knowledgeable about the professions he actually comes close to. Moreover, he creates secondary documents out of the originals, which are appropriately called primary documents. The documentalist translates, analyzes, recopies, photographs, publishes, selects, compares, and coordinates such documents. He is a "team player" in the organization of research and in the implementation of actions that are foundational for a nation. His profession, half intellectual, half manual, is that of an auxiliary to practical research; that is, of being a "servant to the servants of Science."

SIMONS has compared libraries to a storehouse of fertilizers that specialists would be responsible for spreading on the fields so as to make them fertile. We could say that documentalists are the technicians of an improved fertilization of areas that are close or distant from scientific culture. While public reading is for the masses, documentation addresses selected specialists.

Documentary work—based on cultural specialization—corresponds to an activity whose *specificity* no longer has to be demonstrated. What we call "documentary technique" is a combination of techniques that are originally combined and then multiply applied. It goes without saying that one would not require for the student of documentation the curriculum of the École des Chartes[27] and of the Diplôme supérieur de bibliothécaire.[28] If it is necessary to teach cataloging in fifty hours in a library school, one would be satisfied with five hours, for example, in a course designed for documentalists.

The preservation, exhibition, and maintenance of documents will have their place reduced in the curriculum. On the other hand, the standardization, classification, the organization of work within an institution, and the dissemination [of documents] to users, will occupy many more hours than in the neighboring programs.

It is necessary to underline here that the aptitudes and the tasks are not the same at the levels of the assistants and the documentalists; this very useful distinction guides the professional training and the status of assistant documentalists and that of documentalists.

Let us proceed from an analysis of the programs of instruction to an analysis of *the content of the profession.* Instruction pertains to the methods and instruments of documentation. The methods are: standardization, documentary prospecting, bibliography, cataloging, filing, classification, dissemination, and exposition. The instruments or means of documentation are found in the catalog and its cards, files, newspaper clippings, typewriters, calculators, sorting machines, photography, microfilm, and remote transmission [*la télétransmission*].

It happens that the methods of documentary work are borrowed from old or neighboring techniques. All those that one may group under the common heading of collection or conservation, and more particularly, of cataloging, come from pre-documentalist professions. In regard to standardization, or general rationalization, only those specifications recommended in the field of documentation have been kept. Filing and classification are of the greatest importance in the dynamic work of the documentalist. But it is in documentary distribution and what is conventionally called documentary production that there is a genuine professional creation. Orientation toward resources, organizations, and competencies gives to the totality of documentary activities its impulse of a turning wheel and its circular diffusion to the four points of the compass.

Documentary tools, like documentary methods, originate from independent inventions that have found their full employment in the new profession.

Let us now say a word on each of the methods and means that documentation employs.

Standardization has been interested in the methods and means of documentation from the eve of the last war. The International Association of Standards (ISA) has done a study in some of its Bulletins (nos. 22 and 23) on the form of bibliographic references, the presentation of periodicals, the summary of reviews, and the formats of cards and papers. The French Association of Standards [Association Française de Normalisation—AFNOR] has done its own study of the consequences on the national level of directives of the ISA. This effort has led to the establishment in 1940 of the French Commission of Documentation, which having been restructured and subdivided into sections after the war, is dedicated to terminology, bibliographic references, the presentation of periodicals, to the furniture and tools of documentation agencies, and to the presentation of papers.

One subcommittee of the Code of cataloging, located at the Bibliothèque Nationale, has led, with the attentive involvement of librarians, bibliographers, and documentalists, to vast and minute works on the cataloging of common imprints, of engravings, of music, and of geographic maps. Some original texts have been finalized by this commission. Let us name among others: congresses, exhibitions, official publications, posters, and liturgical works. In 1945 AFNOR submitted to public inquiry the first results of this work under the form of a provisionary edition of the *Code* and of important fragments of the presentation of author entries, journal article entries, analytical entries, etc. AFNOR has furthermore accredited a text of Madame CHAUVIN on the rules of the alphabetical arrangement of commercial directories, whose needs are different from those of library catalogs, and whose utilization in banks, industrial, and commercial establishments is now assured. In 1930 the International Institute of Intellectual Cooperation[29] published a Code of periodical title abbreviations that AFNOR adopted for France with some changes in 1944. These different decisions were examined during an international meeting of the ISO (the organization that replaced the ISA) in May 1950. Thanks to an international agreement, some national secretariats have been established in order to solve different issues.

The standardization of card formats has considerably simplified documentary work. Thus, the international card size (75 x 125 [mm]), which is an American invention (NFq 31-003), has now been adopted under the appellation of the library card in all countries, including those that have adopted particular standards for their paper formats. Now, the library card format is a unique format, not related to any initial paper standard. This inconvenience, relating to the French metrical standard (or DIN) dating back to the Convention,[30] did not prevent the United States from creating a union catalog on a continental scale. Photography and microfilm have an equal need for standardization. Central and Northern Europe have understood all the advantages and economy that the metrical format can give them. The formats of French paper NFq 02-001 are similar to the Anglo-Saxon formats without, however, being identical.

Documentary prospecting [*prospection*] is principally performed through bookstores and through bibliography. The book is still the principal source for the research of scholarly documents, and the publisher or bookstore catalogs are the most certain means for detecting interesting works. New and second-hand works are offered in catalogs with their price. Current national bibliographies (*Biblio*,[31] *Bibliography of France*) make known those recent publications that have been legally deposited in the properly designated preservation center. Periodicals as well as books are included. Retrospective, national, or specialized bibliographies, organized by author or by subject, allow research by titles and feature particularities of editions. Periodicals themselves play an important role in discovering new publications by their critical articles and by means of their columns on current bibliography. The indexes or abstracts of periodicals, obtained by the merging and accumulation of the summaries and of tables of contents of these periodicals, allow the easy finding of articles written by a given author or of diverse studies on a particular subject. Sadly, there aren't indexes for all countries, or exhaustive periodical indexes for all disciplines. The International Conference of Bibliography, organized by UNESCO in Paris in November 1950 has noted, among other gaps, the insufficient periodical indexing for the totality of countries represented at the conference.

If the contacts between researchers remain the most vibrant manner for learning about what they're interested in—works in progress, unedited manuscripts, forthcoming works, etc.—*bibliography* is the most important source for information on documentary resources. It is necessary to distinguish three types of instruments: bibliographical catalogs or monographs, reviews of current bibliography, and the great catalogs of libraries. The last ones tend to stand for universal bibliographies. By juxtaposing major catalogs, such as those of the Bibliothèque Nationale in Paris, the British Museum, the Library of Congress, and the Gesamtskatalog [sic],[32] one would approach a universal bibliography. While certain less developed countries did not succeed in including recent publications or national patrimony within their national bibliographies, others, among the greatest, possess catalogs that are bibliographic monuments, by the richness of their content as well as by the scientific character of their descriptive methods.

The entry record in a documentary agency is one thing, the catalog is another. Orderliness demands that every document carry an accession number, which remains attached to it as an unchanging legal identification. And that, moreover, it bear a reference or call number according to a *material classification that allows* it to be found. The topographical catalog follows step by step the arrangement on shelves, in the filing cabinets, and in the binders. Author, title, and subject catalogs allow one to answer diverse questions from patrons: Do such works exist? Under the name of an author? Under a given title? What works can be read on such and such a topic? Alphabetic catalogs are matched up with systematic catalogs where documents are grouped together by cultural affinity. *Catalogs*, as bibliographies, may bring together, in a same alphabetic list, in a same systematic group, diverse documentary formats: books, manuscripts, medals, geographical maps, engravings, photos, and objects. There are catalogs of megalithic stones, stellar spectrums, and epigraphic documents. Documentography is the enumeration and description of diverse documents.

Arranging allows immediate order and permanent storage. Books are not arranged in the same way as when sold in a bookshop, exhibited in an art museum, or when consulted in a specialized library. The use that is intended for the documents, under precise circumstances, determines the type of arrangement. Practical solutions are to be preferred in every case. Nonetheless, arrangement must be distinguished apart from classification. In a museum, arrangement is done and undone according to the needs of the display. In a library, theoretically, volumes have their immutable place, where they return to after having been used.

Concrete classification has to be distinguished from the classification of knowledge. New encyclopedic systems of classification puzzle documentalists, who most often prefer their own classification that fits all their needs. An agency of documentation has a particular point of view in agreement with its own specialization and its peripheral ones, which may be of interest for neighboring disciplines. In this case, it is necessary to build anew a particular classification that takes notice of primary and secondary concerns, inventories all of them, and classifies them in a rational way.

Encyclopedic classifications, which have their direct application in general libraries, can help in constructing concrete classifications—BRUNET[33] inspired many classifications in France during the past hundred years; DEWEY is widely implemented in the Americas. But even with this, the specialists won't be relieved of the task of rethinking every category of their own activity according to existing classes. The development of sciences induces on the one side philosophers and on the other side professionals in documentation to keep encyclopedic classifications up to date. Among the systems that have been of diverse favor in the beginning of the century, the BLISS, the BROWN, the RANGANATHAN, it is necessary to place completely apart the application of the DEWEY decimal system, the famous Universal Decimal Classification, usually called UDC. The Bibliographic Institute of Brussels started it a little more than fifty years ago. An international committee has the responsibility of extending it to new subjects, and of reforming it. It is mainly implemented in central and northern Europe. Nevertheless, France has lined up a growing number of UDC users in the last years, and UFOD, taking over from the French Bibliographic Bureau, recently created a French committee on the Universal Decimal Classification that will have to play its part in the task assumed by the International Federation for Documentation.

The proper job of documentation agencies is to produce secondary documents, derived from those initial documents that these agencies do not ordinarily create, but which they sometimes preserve. Whether these agencies are centers of conservation or whether they intervene as simple users or as relays for the benefit of a category of users, *documentary production* holds a distinctive place within them. We are now at the heart of the documentalist's profession. These secondary documents are called: translations, analyses, documentary bulletins, files, catalogues, bibliographies, dossiers, photographs, microfilms, selections, documentary summaries, encyclopedias, and finding aids. It is necessary to survey the train of documentary tasks, as much as the problems of their development in a world of accelerated technical evolution.

It is no longer necessary to demonstrate the importance of knowing foreign languages for guaranteeing any of the documentary forms. For understanding documents, it is necessary to be able to read them, and today very few subjects are expressed in the linguistic limits of a single language. Thus, it will be the job of the documentalist to deliver to the users documents in diverse languages by the use of high quality *translations*, where there appears a perfect understanding of the subject matter. Nothing is more important, nor so rare, as encountering the cultural specialization of the polyglot; indeed, the project of organizing for France a clearing[34] for translations, that would make available the names of specialists—scientific workers—capable of translating this or that language has been established. Already, the Bureau of Documentation [Direction de la Documentation] for more than the past year has published lists of articles translated under its auspices. In addition, an effort must be made to focus upon the terminology of documentation and its most current productions, the particular terminologies of the most diverse activities as elaborated by the specialists themselves (chemists, doctors, philosophers, bankers, etc.). The glossary of the Librarian will soon appear under the auspices of UNESCO.

The original or translated book needs to be disseminated. It is not enough to translate its title or to assign its principal subject or subjects for a catalog; it is necessary to show its importance in a more or less exhaustive analysis or review. The descriptive reference is accompanied by an analysis that may be short or long. The issue of *documentary analyses* was evoked in 1949 and 1950 at international sessions convened by UNESCO about, first, medicine, then sciences and technology, and eventually, economics and the social sciences. Progress has been made and recommendations have been communicated about the cooperative preparation and standardized presentation of analyses. The coordination of the analyses efforts mentioned in the *Index Bibliographicus*,[35] third edition (first volume in press, second in preparation), is now occurring, thanks to the cooperation of UNESCO, Scientific Associations, and the International Federation for Documentation.

It is sometimes asserted that a single analysis should be sufficient to describe a book, and BRADFORD was no stranger to this trend toward unification, that is to say, non-duplication. This question needs a closer look.

Without speaking about linguistic necessities—a single language cannot address all the world's needs—we must not forget that perspectives change with cultural backgrounds and that the same book will have different uses in a mechanics center or in a hydraulics firm. Far from desiring a single analysis for everyone, it seems that we should consider a short analysis or synopsis for each broad area of activity and a narrowly specialized, functional analysis. The former will occur in publications like the *Bulletin analytique* of the CNRS, the latter one will be the prerogative of very specialized documentary bulletins or in-house bulletins (house organs[36]). Researchers and specialists will be asked an analysis convenient for specific needs. Far from being impersonal and versatile, this latter type of analytic documentation constitutes what we could call the gray matter of documentation agencies.

Descriptive or analytic entries are periodically published in the *Bulletins* of documentation, where, beside various pieces of information, and sometimes leading articles, all that is useful to a professional or scientific activity is distributed to the users. Bulletins ordinarily depend on the classification of the publishing agency. Headings may or may not be numbered. Documentary elements are to be retrieved or not in an index at the end of each issue or in a cumulative index. Notes may or may not be cut off, to be inserted in a file. Bulletins communicate to the users, near or far, a documentation that one could call predigested.

Let us return to the description or mark-up of documents. These notes have to be extremely mobile, able to be classified according to the needs of a desired order, and to be interfiled without delay in series that are instantly extensible. These needs lie at the origin of the invention of the *card* [*fiche*], which exists in many formats, adopted for use or standardized in certain countries. The most well-known filing card is called the international filing card. Its dimensions are often too small for certain uses. One can double it or increase it tenfold to enlarge the original. Directories present a different attraction than card catalogs, for, though they don't allow interfiling, they do offer the advantage of being consultable at a distance. *Catalogs* encompass periods or limited series: they are assembled by accumulation or by the merger of card catalogs. They include indexes when systematic. Still, the most widely spread is that of alphabetic order, organized by authors, titles, or subjects. *Cataloging*, "ars catalogandi," is at the heart of the librarian's profession, who is often guided in his or her work by cataloging rules that are specific to an establishment, type of library, country, or group of countries. We have seen that a French cataloging code for librarians, bibliographers, and documentalists, was being prepared by AFNOR, in collaboration with the Bibliothèque Nationale. The Anglo-American Code[37] and the Vatican

Library cataloging rules codify the Anglo-Saxon approach. The codification extends to more and more documentary forms: books, engravings, maps, photographs, recorded disks, art works, bookbinding, book-plates, museum collections, patents, etc. The establishment of *tables of contents* and *indexes* deserves a place in professional education.

Catalogs inform us as to the location of documents for purchasing, consulting, or borrowing. Bibliographies inform us as to the choices that are available in regard to such and such a book in relation to a given subject. *Documentographies* extend the field of this selection. Bibliographies, in contrast to catalogs, are classified according to a rational order, chronological or systematic. In order to be satisfactory, the bibliography, just as the documentography, must be constructed—in respect to the norms of presentation or the forms of the entries—by the collection specialists. Bibliography operates by selection and elimination, according to a hierarchical order. It is accompanied or not by judgments of value.

The *orientation* or localization of documents is done by union catalogs. The orientation or information on the proper topic of the documents is performed by abstracts, documentary bulletins, and bibliographies that are of interest to the specialists of the subject, which may be, according to the publication format, very vast or slim. The orientation of agencies and competencies is assured by guides which, when they take on the orientation of documents themselves and of bibliography, give unanimist[38] publications, such as the MANUELS DE LA RECHERCHE DOCUMENTAIRE published by the French Union of Documentation Organizations [UFOD]; GÉOGRAPHIE, under the direction of M. Emm. de MARTONNE; PHILOSOPHIE, under the direction of M. R. BAYER; SCIENCES ECONOMIQUES (in preparation) under the direction of M. Ch. MORAZÉ. It is to be wished that, following the example of France, other countries reveal to researchers their documentary resources. This is the resolution adopted by the International Conference of Documentation held at Oxford in 1938.

The documentary orientation can correct what may sometimes be too narrow about specialization in its depth. The documentalist, much more than the researcher, needs to open the windows of his specialization to a horizon without limits. This "biased" dynamism of constantly surveying the extent of its specialization corresponds to that which an author has justly called the documentalist "*attitude*," or still yet, the professional comportment of a documentalist. It is known that only 30 percent of the useful documentation produced in a documentary service is related to the specialization of the agency itself.

Thus, we now perceive two tendencies: with librarians, the concern is that of producing card catalogs, and consequently increasingly vast, almost universal union catalogs which are able to respond to the question: where can one find a particular work, a rare edition?—without respect to the subject involved. On the other side, with documentalists, there is an effort to prospect and divulge the very diverse means of access to multiform documents, with the means specific to each discipline. These two tendencies correspond to the specialty of the professions: the former is essentially related to the form of documents, the latter is centered on the cultural or functional specialization. The researchers and scholars find their rewards in these two enterprises of current awareness and orientation.

The first activities are more traditional than those of documentation. Only orientation ensures the transition.

For the past few centuries, the book has remained *the bibliographic entity*. Autographs were grouped within books. Engravings were preserved within albums. Periodicals were bound in volumes. Today, books have a tendency to become scattered in loose leaves. The book accompanies the scholar's notepad. The publishing business reconsiders its methods for best responding to the demand of the century.

For some decades, the fact, information, the periodical text, the illustration have been isolated from their contexts: pulled from the book, the daily paper, the periodical, the official newspaper, and given a place in *binders*. By an inverse evolution of the card catalog, which schematizes and brings together descriptions of documents, the construction of such binders tends to present the documents themselves, assembling them for ease of consultation. This happens in the majority of cases with graphic documents. It is nevertheless possible to find in binders an example, a specimen, of a given matter.

Next to filing cards and catalogs which present the schematized picture of documents through an abstract description of their formal aspect, accompanied or not by a photograph, one may now notice parallel catalogs obtained by the codification of elements that enables statistics or selection. Here, the word disappears and even the letter is absent, as we are dealing with perforated card machines. Statistical *data-processing* [*mécanographie*] gets us accustomed to replicating the cards that are legible with cards in which each mark is a conventionally agreed upon translation for the directly intelligible signs. The progress of cybernetics, especially at the Massachusetts Institute of Technology, links the complicated precision of an already old automatism to the flashy quickness of more effective electro-technical applications. The documentalist will be more and more dependent upon tools whose technicality increases with great rapidity. "Homo documentator" must prepare himself to take command—with all his senses awake—over the robots of tomorrow. The value of the machine will be that of a servant. "Our ability to overtake machinism lies in our possibilities of assimilating the machine" (MUMFORD[39]).

The hand copy, the mold, the sketch, the painting of an object— landscapes or fortifications—remain *means for the reproduction of documents*. To these old processes are more recently added the copying of letters, tracing, typewriting, Roneo duplication, silk-screen printing, Lumitype[40] xerography,[41] office tools such as Ormo, Everest, etc. . . . , and in the last few years— related to photography—the ozalid and entocé processes, etc. . . . , where transparencies play a new role. Each of these processes should be studied in regard to its cost of production and the use that can be made of it in a particular case.

Photocopying on plates, film, and rolls has become the principal aid of documentary production. Black and white photos, photos directly produced on paper, black and white or color facsimiles, reproductions to size, enlargements, blow-ups, negatives, and positives increase the possibility of examination at a distance and the permanent examination of initial and derived documents.

The use of perforated or imperforated 35 mm *microfilm* has been a giant step in documentary technique. In documentary agencies, photographic and microfilm services have carried out the wishes of the users and they have profoundly modified the style and speed of internal work. For the convenience of classification and consulting, the microfilm roll—in an evolution that is analogous to that which we talked of about the book—has been broken apart into cuttings or strips of images, which can be stored in sized envelopes, classified by titles and subjects. These documentary copies demand, however, tools for reading: pocket magnifying glasses, wall or ceiling projectors, readers, and searching machines. Some excellent tools of this sort carry the names of THOMSON, DE BRIE, CORDONNIER.[42] After a long evolution, the electronic microscope takes its place beside the primitive magnifying glass.

Television makes its appearance in the *telescript*, which allows one to transmit and transcribe a document from a distance, at the same size or enlarged four times maximum. The transmitter is the size of an upright piano; the reception is performed by 120 lines on a chemically treated paper that is unwound up to the final operation of quick-drying it. Documentary television will, furthermore, allow for more supple documentary cinematography by giving to users, or television viewers, possibilities for study that could not happen in cinemas.

Thus, documentary techniques very clearly mark two distinct tendencies. The first is toward an always increasingly abstract and algebraic schematization of documentary elements (catalogs, codes, perforations, classifications through conventionally agreed upon marks). The second is toward a massive extension of "substitutes for lived experiences" (photos, films, television, audio records, radio broadcasting). The point of application for these techniques is of interest not only for a profession that is increasingly aware, but also for an ever-growing audience—the innumerable masses—that education, the press, and propaganda investigate, enroll, and capture thanks to their attractive or demonstrative character. What words fail to communicate, image and sound try to deliver to all. Documentation, thus understood, is a powerful means for the *collectivization of knowledge and ideas*.

All professions have their executives and their assistants. *The documentary profession* is no exception. Hardly freed from the older professions of librarian, archivist, and collection curator, it is obliged to seek comparisons within education, commerce, and industry. More or less manual, according to the position in a hierarchy, it is partly intellectual, partly technical at every level. The documentalist is a specialized technician, whose professional knowledge will be increasingly technical in the future. However, one must thoroughly insist on the importance of cultural specialization in the staffing of the profession. Whereas, by definition, documentary assistants are polyvalent and can easily take with them their technical competencies from one documentary agency to the next, documentalists must select, understand, translate, interpret, and utilize—in the intellectual sense of the word—those documents which they have authority over, in accordance with the specialty of their agency. Therefore, cultural specialization for the documentalist is more important than for those professions that preserve documents.

This is why the *aptitudes and qualifications* that are required of the documentation agency *heads and their assistants* are not identical. The documentary assistant must be careful, meticulous, with a hand always ready to put things in place; he must love order, know the handling of machines and tools, know typing, have a certain rapidity, an above average efficiency, a certain elementary education, good spelling, an inclination toward arranging, and last, docility. One expects much more of the documentalist. First of all, [he must have] an internal understanding of the specialty which is the object of the organization's proper activities (chemistry, forestry, pedagogy, engineering, gas meters, glass making, textile industry, domestic arts, whatever may be the case). Then, a doctrinal preparation applied to the methods and techniques of documentation. It is necessary to know at least two foreign languages, also. Last, the documentalist must have the ability to organize and direct things and people, shown through the following qualities: order, clear headedness, psychology, anticipation, invention, consistency, social sense, and authority.

The *functioning of a documentation center* is largely made up of managerial methods that connect this activity to the organization of work. Without personal and collective organization, there is no smooth functioning. Finances, equipment, tools, publications, distribution, advertising, manpower, choice of personnel, and external relations—these are the principal concerns of the head documentalist. The multiple problems that affect the work of a documentation center have been discussed in a manual published in Paris in 1946 by the three institutes specializing in rubber, citrus fruits, and oils and oleaginous. One can find in this work excellent advice and tips, some of which are particular to the organizations in question, but which open the way to a systematization of methods and doctrines as regards to professional documentary work.

In specialized centers and departments, documentation is delivered without delay or it is deferred. It is produced on demand or it is spontaneously distributed. In the first case, it is made to conform to individual needs. In the second case, it anticipates the needs of groups of workers. In all cases, the power of selection comes fully into play, and it is here that the most important abilities of the documentalist come into play—that is to say—innate knowledge of the subject, impartiality, and a sense of the connection between documents. Selection for individual or collective use is the particular task of the professional documentalist.

Thus, the components of the profession seem to be: collectivization, specialization, coordination, documentary reproduction, distribution, complete management, codification, selection, individualization, and economy.

The acquisition and set-up of documentation [translators' note: that is, of documentation centers] is costly. At first glance, they don't seem to make any difference. But from a higher perspective, the work of a documentation service is seen to be beneficial to the administrative, the technical, and the scientific activities upon which an organization depends. In fact, this work is *profitable*, on condition, of course, that it is conducted by the masterly hands of professional documentalists.

This is an essential quality upon which one cannot insist strongly enough in the practice of the profession: the dynamism of documentation. An English colleague has tried to characterize documentary activity by reducing it to what could be termed an "attitude." While this simplification, by its very nature, conceals the complexity of documentary tasks—as a galloping horse placing itself between the spectators and the herd that it belongs to—it is true that the documentalist does not view documents as if he was simply responsible for receiving them, numbering them, classifying and transmitting them, a task that is more static, yet sometimes surpassed by the nonpassive processes of acquisitions choice and indexing by subjects. We have to emphasize that the documentalist spirit can renew the oldest concepts of preservation. Libraries themselves can only draw great profit by the most efficient application of contemporary documentology. On the other hand, documentalists have much to learn from their "elders" of neighboring professions, in which sometimes age-old experience has been deposited in proven practices. These reciprocal responses should be very beneficial to both public culture and to professional advancement.

Schools for documentalists are rare. France has advanced considerably in this area. The separate education which the UFOD established in 1945 has some original curricula with a great degree of specificity. It is essentially characterized by subjects specific to the professional education in question, and by a particular degree of common topics shared between several neighboring fields. Within the former, we find classification, analysis, patents, the international organization of documentation, types of users, the listing of administrative documents, specialized documentation and its varied resources, the creation of documents, documentography. Shared topics occupy a much more modest place in the programs of the UFOD: the recording and preservation of documents, bibliography, cataloging, librarianship, archival work, museum studies, publishing, and management. The Technical Courses of Documentation, which corresponded to the middle and higher levels of this professional education, have been joined to the Conservatoire National des Arts et Métiers by order of the Ministry for Technical Education dated December 1, 1950, under the name of the Institut National des Techniques de la Documentation. The official curriculum is essentially targeted to the education of documentalists in industrial and commercial organizations. During the first year, nevertheless, it holds a "propaedeutic" [preparatory] value, thanks to instruction about common techniques and methods regardless of cultural specialization. This first year is thus a kind of preamble to the specialized instruction of the second year, which involves an immersion in a climate of methodological or technical research that ought to continuously raise the level [of instruction] in relation to invention, organization, and applied psychology.

[*Translators' Note*: Because of word processing limitations, we have had to slightly modify the exact, original appearance of Briet's chart.]

Technicians	Priority of Qualifications		
	I	II	III
Technicians (Operators/ Technical aids)	Primary or secondary education	Elementary technique of document handling	Elementary technique of document use and production
Archivists, Librarians, Collection curators	Higher education and general knowledge	Technique of document handling (history, preservation, communication)	Cultural specialization
Documentalists	Higher education and cultural or professional specialization	Technique of document use and production	Technique of document handling

Versatility			Specialization		
T	T		T		
	A			A	
	L			L	
	C			C	
		D		D	D

T = Technicians
A = Archivists
L = Librarians
C = Collections curators
D = Documentalists

III. A Necessity of Our Time

For Charles LE MAISTRE [43]

There exist a certain number of *agencies of documentation* which are *closed* to the public and which resort to a self-sufficiency that is beneficial to their own activity. These are, first of all, industrial and commercial services that fear external competition and which jealously protect themselves against potential pillage. There are also military or technical services working with national defense, which have received orders of secrecy. These agencies are usually well informed, for, while they make their documentation available to a limited number of users, they nonetheless largely open it to both the most remote and the most narrowly specialized investigations. Among the first, we will cite, as an example, the chemical and technical Documentation department of Saint-Gobain glass trade, the Association of Heavy Industries, the

Documentation department of the Technical Institute for Studies and Research on Lipids. Among the second may be cited the Documentation and Technical Information Department of Aeronautics and the Documentation Center for Atomic Energy.

However, most centers and departments are almost completely *open* to the public. The formalities of admission allow various accommodations. In this case, documentation is innately generous. There would be a long list of all the French successes that might be praised. Let us mention only the French Petroleum Institute, the Technical Center of Aluminum, the National Center of Telecommunications, the Technical Office of Printing, the National Foundation of Political Sciences, the Documentation department of the state-controlled Renault Factory, the Bureau of Financial Studies of Crédit Lyonnais, the Meter Manufacturing Company. Other documentation agencies are in one way or another intermediaries, using the documentation of other agencies and specializing in the distribution of facts or documentary elements of all types. One may compare these *user* agencies to "relays." For these, more than for the closed centers, the organization of work and classification plays a central role in the arrangement of deliverable services. Whether they may be an agency or a scientific review such as the *Intermédiaire des Recherches Mathématiques* or an encyclopedic center of information such as SVP,[44] the relays play the role of distributors of documentation.

The *centers* of documentation, properly speaking, are the source of documentary materials. They produce secondary documents, elaborated from the initial documents. They are organized as factories, with their documentary chain of production. They investigate the complete field of a specialty, taking their share in publications in every language and every country. They keep for their direct users, insiders or outsiders, the initial documents that they have gathered, and the secondary documents or "by-products" which they have developed. This type of agency tends to assert itself with the growth of a national or international organization, which we will have to consider. Let us cite the examples of the Chemistry Center [Maison de la Chimie], the Natural History Museum [Muséum d'Histoire Naturelle], the Mechanics Documentation Center [Centre de Documentation de la Mécanique], and the Building Trade Information and Documentation Center [Centre d'Information et de Documentation du Bâtiment].

Beyond these centers, it is still necessary to distinguish what one could call the general *offices* of official character or —if they are still private—on the way to being nationalized. The offices create or edit documents. They also assure the complete as possible collection of documentation relative to their sector of activity. One recognizes in them, as well, the task of distribution. Only rarely do they have direct contact with the users. Very frequently they are born from the combined efforts of trade unions, associations, and departmental or local services, which organized themselves toward better control of their collections and in the technique of documentary delivery.[45] In this manner the Bureau of Documentation creates documents of great informational value. The journal *Inter-technique* distributes translations that are made by specialists in different fields. The Academic Bureau for Professional Statistics and Documentation [Bureau Universitaire de Statistique et de Documentation Professionnelles] distributes to its Parisian and departmental branches all the scholarly information that needs to be conveyed to the students. The National Federation of Social Security Agencies [Fédération Nationale des Organismes de Sécurité Sociale] works for its constituents. The Documentation Department of O.E.C.E.[46] is at the exclusive disposal of the United Nations and of the Economic Organization of the Marshall Plan.

The Centers and the Departments of documentation that are open draw their public's attention through advertising, as commercial businesses do, and through enlisting themselves in guides on documentary agencies. They form associations between themselves, as they have done in France, Great Britain, Belgium, etc., for the study and teaching of common methods. They constitute the national network of documentation, a network that is still too wide-meshed, sometimes broken, and sometimes inexplicably fastened. From all sides, the need is felt to organize documentary chaos. Centers and departments multiply. ROSSELLO[47] justly speaks of "budding," this symptomatic activity that announces a manifest state. One must not speak too fast of an overlapping in documentary activities. For it is very rare that a given activity would not organically distinguish itself from some other activity with which one would like to see it combine. If we take, for example, the cinema, it would become clear to us that there is room for several agencies of documentation: the technique (production), the profession (unions), and the historical (preservation and study). The forms that documentary work assumes are as numerous as the needs from which they are born.

One could ask if documentary services may not one day transform themselves into *public services*, just as with civil engineering, mail, and public education. This anticipation helps us to see, rising on the horizon of our civilization, a sort of nationalization of cultural information. Already, the Bureau of Documentation, attached to the Government [*la Présidence du Conseil*], has carved out an official domain in the Information sector. Other territories will be conquered one after another, as the authorities become gradually aware of their responsibilities in matters of documentation organization.

Some considerable collections are on their way. We can think, for example, of the population census, of registry office services, of official statistics, of all types of printed matter that the agents of the S.N.C. F.[48] receive, of the military and industrial mobilizations, of the managed supply of food—all mass activities which demand large scale documentary tools regulated by the State.

A while ago, somebody suggested that administrative documentation be organized at the cantonal level (M. POUTEAU, Congress of 1937).[49] Some years later, this idea gave birth to an attempt to regulate the administrative services of prefectures and subprefectures. In the same vein, exploited step by step, we have to point out M. DAYRE's project of assuring the exhaustive analysis of the *Journal Officiel de la République Française* by a central service. Always at a national level, at a quick pace, centers of documentation were created over the past two years in the departmental Archives. Under the initiative of the Director of the French Archives, CHARLES BRAIBANT, 32 centers have been established which, connected to a university or municipal library, the academy, societies of scholars, chambers of commerce, and prefect's offices, are capable of providing current documentation of a legislative, administrative, economic, political, or cultural character. This way the French network is being built, link after link. Furthermore, documents are drawn into vast reservoirs, the centers of preservation, collecting at length, inevitably, all that constitute national heritage, the commonplace and the extremely rare, journals as much as the most precious treasures. Museums, libraries, and archives are growing without measure, raising problems of organization and current awareness. Diverse forms of documents may be sometimes encountered in them with certain overlaps that tend to become more pronounced over time: one finds artistic bookbindings and miniatures in certain museums, libraries preserve archives of historic interest and collectable objects; official publications or modern archival pieces are most often printed or typed, and microfilm is everywhere. Between the State establishments, there is a sort of competition for the delimitation of activities. The authorities must now proceed to the allocation of collections, to the inventory of specialized collections in diverse domains, and to the regulation of documentary offices in public establishments.

Already, some ministerial or interministerial *commissions* have been created in France for reviewing central administrative activities in matters of documentation (1946), or to coordinate the official activities (Decree of December 30, 1950). The French *Committee* of Documentation, created in 1938–1939 and reformed in 1951 under the presidency of M. Julien CAIN, administrator of the Bibliothèque Nationale, in view, principally, of ensuring the representation of French documentation in foreign countries, constitutes the French Section of the International Federation for Documentation. Since 1932 the French *Union* of Documentation Organizations has brought together in an association governed by the law of 1901[50] central offices, centers, official and private documentation departments, as well as documentary technicians across all categories. Otherwise, certain documentary enterprises are gathered together in a typical *Employer's Union*. We see appearing elements of a general organization of French documentation in which the National Center of Scientific *Research* [Centre National de la *Recherche* Scientifique] should play a role, with its analytical Bulletin and its groups of scientific workers, recognized by specialties. It should, therefore, have a more richly endowed budget.

The structure of the *national organization* of documentation, previously considered as a more or less public service, varies with the country. In the United States where very great institutions set the example, such as the Army Medical Library or the United States Department of Agriculture, it is increasingly acknowledged that part of the state's job is to take the lead of the movement toward a better documentary organization" (*sic*[51]) (SHERA[52]). In countries that tend toward totalitarianism, as in Hungary today, until recently documentation had its official centers, rigorously state controlled. But in the Anglo-Saxon world, it seems that the current terminology shackles the evolution of ideas, and consequently, of organizing activity. The terms "special librarian," "library," and "bibliography"[53] have different meanings than in our country, where we have the neologisms made necessary by the present situation, and where "documentalist," "documentation center," and "documentography" correspond to a state that is, if not more advanced, at least more theoretically elaborated.

M. Luther EVANS[54] has done a very acute critique of the insufficiencies which come about in certain agencies when the users' needs are ignored: "I have the deep conviction that the library services that we know are performed according to the needs of subject specialists, while they should be 'made to order' for the researchers of the industry that is directly concerned." Indeed, it is true that the rigidity of classifications, the lack of flexibility in the methods, and the petty bureaucrats among the personnel constitute permanent dangers in libraries and agencies alike. The solution to this problem will be eventually found in the way of personnel recruitment, that is to say, in an appropriate professional education.

In the most advanced countries, one is more or less clearly aware of the current needs of nationally organized documentation. Also, it is not difficult to speak the same language to those, pioneers or zealots, who gather together at international conferences. The International Federation for Documentation, seated in The Hague, convenes yearly meetings attended by delegates from 20 national sections (Germany, Belgium, China, Denmark, Spain, the USA, Finland, France, Great Britain, Hungary, Indonesia, Italy, Japan, Netherlands, Portugal, Romania, Sweden, Switzerland, Czechoslovakia, South Africa) and by the correspondents of many other countries. Successor to the IIB[55] (1895), this famous institution in Brussels, which produced the UDC and the Répertoire Bibliographique, the FID has two incontestable fiefs. These are the universal decimal classification and the technical methods of documentation. On other issues, such as bibliographical reference, professional education, abstracting, archives, and bibliography, a competition occurs with neighboring organizations, such as the International Federation of Library Associations (F.I.A.B. or I.F.L.A.) [Fédération Internationale des Associations de Bibliothécaires], the Council of Scientific Associations [Conseil des Unions Scientifiques], and the International Council of Archives [Conseil International des Archives].

Since the Second World War, UNESCO has played the chief role in assembling and energizing experts and organizations in the educational and cultural field. Its Division of Libraries, under the direction of Edw. CARTER, has systematically pursued, in relation to other sections of UNESCO, a cultural policy that guarantees that its current results will be passed onto the future. "The living republic of minds" (J. TORRES-BODET[56]) is being created through a subterranean evolution with the United Nations as the temporary perhaps, but useful, frame. Some outposts of scientific cooperation (Manila, Delhi, Cairo, Montevideo) are points of departure for missionaries of a new type, charged with the cultural development of the more or less uncultured masses and with multiplying contacts with scholars. The technical assistants of UNESCO, in fact, have available a sometimes immense "hinterland" to explore and organize. It is through reciprocal actions and reactions that these outposts spread out and are scientifically informed. The battle against illiteracy, the organization of a reading public, of librarianship, and of documentation in all its forms, comes in the wake of this exploration vessel flying the United Nations flag. The UNESCO vouchers, this new currency, are valid in 21 countries and through the outposts of scientific cooperation for obtaining not only all books and similar documents, but even microfilms and scientific materials. Interlibrary solidarity has been demonstrated over the past year by the aid that young and efficient Danish librarians have given to the damaged library of Valognes.[57] UNESCO manuals make available to everyone, in two or three languages, proven methods of library services (Mc COLVIN) and of professional teaching (DANTON). The Archives have announced the second edition of their international catalog of inventories. ICOM[58] has organized at UNESCO an information center on every kind of collection. M.L. EVANS has proposed the reduction of worldwide copyright centers from 75 to five.

This partial unification, which is one step in an absolute unification that has been impossible to realize up to the present time, is arduous in our divided world. It has become commonplace, however, to affirm that humanity strives toward *unity*. The historical sketch that Paul PERRIER[59] has given of this evolution over the centuries is striking. He insists on the ineluctability of the law of unification that he has discovered in his patient, historical work. He explains the success and failure of regressive or progressive human enterprises. He has put into perspective the role of international relations in our time: "International relations and influences justly figure to be among the most important facts of universal history. Their importance is multiplied in the modern period. It is more than a question of exchanges, of relations, it is an intimate solidarity. . . . Our universe makes up a whole. . . . The likenesses between different human societies have grown stronger during the last half century in all areas, in spite of ideological battles, world wars, and opposing interests. This likeness is not only explicable, as in ancient times, by the idea of needs, but it is a result of the conscious and systematic imitation of the foreign. Universal suffrage, compulsory schooling, the battle against epidemics, the progress of feminism, social laws, the organization of work, constitutions and political parties—all these social phenomena are the result of imitation, as much as of economic necessity. International influences are no longer events, episodes; they depend on genuine official institutions, they are linked to thousands of establishments. Most states are no longer represented to other states by ambassadors and consuls only, but by associations, schools, and institutes too, whose mission simultaneously involves understanding foreign civilizations and disseminating through the world the language, works, and civilizations of their own countries. . . . International relations are so essential in contemporary civilization that this term 'influence,' which marked past results, has become no longer sufficient. They are on the way to realizing that yearning of human societies for thousands of years . . . 'this immeasurable unity, up until now unreachable by empires, religions, and philosophies.'"

The principal obstacle to unification lies in the multiplicity of languages, in the babelism that stands in opposition to both understanding and cooperation. One almost no longer seeks to substitute an artificial language for natural ones. Esperanto isn't progressing. On the contrary, the major languages, that is to say, English, French, and Spanish, tend to spread so as to become the indispensable interpreters of civilized people. German has retreated. Russian is not yet in the forefront. The Orientals always speak their language and another language. The world divides itself into linguistic areas. The organization of documentary work must take account of this reality. In regard to the creation of cataloging rules, book selection, translations, and analyses, the distribution of documents on the planet will adapt to this necessity. The recording of linguistic phenomena is not of any less importance than the recording of illiteracy statistics.

Documentology addresses itself to remedying linguistic confusion. Numeric or alphanumeric classifications are artificial languages applied to knowledge or to documents. The codes applied to mechanical duplication are internationally valid too. Standard languages are beginning to stand out in regard to synopses of authors or translations of documentary analyses.

We must distinguish two tendencies at play today. On the one hand, knowledge of foreign languages allows a much larger diffusion of written works than previously, and gives to worldwide readership an audience that can only increase. One thinks of the innumerable translations of the Bible, Victor Hugo, Marx, and Duhamel. On the other hand, the scientific work of documentation tends to content itself with a few base languages for reasons of economy. The scientific translation ought to be organized with as much care as the literary translation. While individually, one seeks direct contact with, or multiple translations of, literary monuments of every country and of all times, collectively, the technique of document distribution will be content with three or four languages, maximum.

The schematic or iconographic description of documents is enlarging. Union catalogs begin to take into account *geographical areas* that are sometimes linked to linguistic areas. Some of them have attained continental proportions. One can foresee that with or without the standardization of entries one will have in the not so distant future the possibility of internationally orienting researchers of documents. The international directories and specialized guides *already* take part in this global orientation.

Documentary research, as applied to tasks of schoolwork, should be brought into compulsory and free schooling. For, it is not just sufficient to read for the purpose of understanding; one must also know how to find and utilize documents. The dynamism of living documentation joins with the dynamism of the mind seeking truth. It is here that one can justly speak of "breathless striving" in designating this urgent need of the mind. At all *educational* levels, documentary method must be universally and widely instilled in persons and in teams. The *professional education* of documentalists poses an additional problem of an international character: the systems, methods, and achievements must be compared to one another within a high-level international institute, open to experts and teachers of documentary technique.

We have left for the end an essential feature of documentary effectiveness —we want to speak about "public relations," those human relations that have been made much of on both sides of the Atlantic and which are studied in our country under the rubric of *"human issues"* [*problèmes humains*]. Human issues are always present in documentary activities. Altruism, team spirit, managerial aptitude, user psychology, capacity to adapt to the needs of a group, to the needs of individual researchers, social sense, affability, readiness to help, and zeal in research—these are many of the signs of the extroverted attitude of the documentalist. These optimal qualities give to the profession its social and progressive character, which saves it from mechanization and an excessive specialization. A human type that is particularly dynamic starts to be encountered everywhere: knowledgeable, methodological, efficient, and sociable. One could cite numerous and engaging examples of specimens among documentary technicians and scientific workers. Thanks to them, intellectual egoism is regressing and friendship makes its way into intellectual work. Others are attracted to the richness of the documentary experience.

A diagram that has become classic among documentalists has made clear to the eyes and to the mind three levels upon which, little by little, *the international network of documentation* has come to be realized. The horizontal plane is that of the geographical areas where one sees local, regional, national, and international organizations. The vertical plane is that of specialties, whose aggregation produces encyclopedic forms, of agencies of all orders, more widely and more finely realized. The third level or diagonal plane depicts the associations and federations of documentary technicians. One could also depict these three aspects of the international organization of documentation by an armillary sphere of three turning rings that embrace our globe, the Earth. In spite of conflicts in documentary activities, of still numerous gaps, one can already see the international organization that is called to play the role of being the motor and governor of relations and researchers. The apparatus is in place. It is only necessary to activate it. This will be the job of good-willed men and professional activists who are closely or distantly associated with documentary activities. On the horizontal plane, creations are expected at the local level, and overall, at the national level. On the vertical plane, concentrations are developing little by little. On the diagonal plane, coordination has been started between the federations, though this does not exclude the decentralization of certain responsibilities.

"Against the disarray of the universe, today one can only count on the miracles of the will, born of an irreducible belief in the future of culture."

Thus, said Ventura Garcia CALDERON to the readers of the *Deux-Mondes*[60] in February 1951. Indeed, the more the innumerable and uncultured masses arise from freed areas, the more it is necessary to instruct, enlighten, and culturally assist them.[61]

The time is past—it was 1931—when an English librarian said at an international conference that if he would mention documentation in his country he would be asked what this new disease might be.

The words, doctrines, techniques, and tools have forged a path. Theory and practice have kept pace. The new profession has become more and more technical: learned on the one hand, manual on the other. "What a manual century!"[62] RIMBAUD said, speaking of his own, nineteenth, century. While culture was being democratized, technology was making gigantic progress. The means of expression multiplied while expanding their range in space and time. Expositions and congresses thwarted the tendency of all specializations, just as all frontiers, to withdraw within themselves. The appreciation of human unity has been growing on cultural, political, social, and religious fronts.

Documentation-technique, the documentation-profession, and the documentation-institution are not enough to address all the needs of the growing society. They are, nonetheless, essential mechanisms that must, henceforth, be reckoned with.

February 28, 1951

Notes

1. Julien Cain was the general administrator at the French National Library (Bibliothèque Nationale) and, thus, Suzanne Briet's supervisor while she was employed there as a librarian.

2. (1898–1959). Philosopher. At that time, chair of aesthetics and the sciences of art at Sorbonne University.

3. French National Bibliography. Bibliography of France was its name until 1990.

4. "Graphic documents" translates *documents graphiques* and, as is clear from the beginning of Briet's text and from the history of documentation up to her time, the term "*graphiques*" refers to all manners of documentary inscription: written, pictorial, sound, and so on.

5. (1899–1977). Teacher at the INTD (Institut National des Techniques de la Documentation), specializing in bibliography.

6. Henry Bliss (1870–1955). Librarian at the College of the City of New York and author of the Bliss classification system (1910).

7. Neologism. Information science.

8. Neologism. "Documentography is the enumeration and description of diverse documents," chapter II.

9. Proverbial: poor, but happy.

10. The Periodical Department of the Bibliothèque Nationale.

11. Briet's point here is that humanists need a "thread" of past, historical documents in order to bring the past into the present.

12. Robert Pagès (1919–present) graduated in philosophy in 1942 and was an influential young leftist in Toulouse and in Paris. He met Suzanne Briet after the war at the Bibliothèque Nationale and followed the courses at the UFOD. In 1948 he wrote a memoir where he stressed the cultural power of documentation: "Problèmes de classification culturelle et documentaire." Teaching a course about classification at the INTD from 1950 to 1957, he invented "coded analysis," an artificial language of indexation, to fulfill the documentary needs of the Laboratory of Social Psychology at the Sorbonne, which he founded and headed from 1951 to 1985. See *Documentaliste* 29 (2), March–April, 1992: "Robert Pagès et l'analyse codée," by André Demailly.

13. Andrew Carnegie (1835–1919). A rich philanthropist who helped create free public libraries in the English-speaking world.

14. English in the original.

15. Centre National de la Recherche Scientifique, Paris, founded in 1939.

16. This firm still exists in Grenoble, as a part of the Alstom group. It is now called "Alstom Hydro Power."

17. Henri Verne was in 1937 the head of French museums and a member of the International Committee of Documentation.

18. Eugene Wigner (1902–1995). Hungarian-American physicist.

19. John Ely Burchard (1898–1975). Professor at MIT.

20. English in the original.

21. (1901–1960). French nuclear physicist.

22. Paul Le Rolland. Scientist and communist, he was director of French technical education (1944–1947).

23. (1887–1975). British biologist and author.

24. English in the original.

25. Louis Ragey headed CNAM (Conservatoire National des Arts et Métiers), on which depended and still depends the INTD (Institut national des techniques de la documentation), which Briet helped create.

26. English in the original.

27. École des Chartes: a prestigious French "grande école" for archivists, founded in 1821, where students are taught to decipher and to keep ancient documents. Its programs include intensive studies in Medieval Latin and medieval history.

28. Diplôme Supérieur de Bibliothécaire: an academic degree for librarians, equivalent to five years of university study. This degree no longer exists in the university. The reference librarian training school is now the Enssib (École Normale Supérieure des Sciences de l'Information et des Bibliothèques) founded in 1992, replacing the Ensb (École Nationale Supérieure de Bibliothécaire, founded in 1963).

29. The International Institute of Intellectual Cooperation, founded in 1926, belonged to the Society of Nations. It was replaced in 1945 by UNESCO. (See Sylvie Fayet-Scribe, *Histoire de la documentation en France: culture, science et technologie de l'information: 1895–1937* (Paris: CNRS Éditions, 2000), 72.)

30. The French Convention (1792–1795).

31. "Biblio" is the name of a French bibliography created in the thirties by Eric de Grolier (1911–1998), a documentation pioneer. (See Fayet-Scribe, *Histoire de la documentation en France*, 160.)

32. German National Bibliography until World War II: Preußischer Gesamtkatalog (circa 1900–1935), then Deutscher Gesamtkatalog (1935–1945). (See Bibliothekskennzeichnung in Deutschland by Andreas Heise, www.ib.hu-berlin.de/~kumlau/handreichungen/h60/.)

33. Charles-Jacques Brunet, 1780–1867, French bookseller and bibliographer.

34. English in the original. Briet may have meant "clearing house."

35. A publication of FID (International Federation for Documentation).

36. English in the original. "House organs" are internal bulletins for an organization.

37. English in the original. The Anglo-American Code of cataloging was first published in 1908.

38. Unanimism: Nineteenth-century literary movement founded by Jules Romains, based on group consciousness and collective feelings.

39. Lewis Mumford (1895–1990), author of *Technics and Civilization* (New York: Harcourt Brace, 1934) and author of the concept of the "Megamachine."

40. Photocomposition.

41. An ancestor of photocopying. The word remains in "Xerox," the famous firm.

42. From Gérard Cordonnier, a French engineer, inventor of the Selecto system.

43. British engineer and cofounder of ISO (1946).

44. S'il Vous Plait: a corporate information phone service.

45. The French, here, is unclear: ". . . qui se sont groupés pour mieux dominer, et leurs collections, et la technique de la distribution de la documentation."

46. L'Organisation Européenne de Coopération Économique. Part of the Marshall Plan, now l'Organisation de Coopération et de Développement Économiques (OCDE).

47. Pedro Rossello (1929–1970). Assistant director of the International Bureau of Education (UNESCO). For details, see www.ibe.unesco.org/International/DocServices/Recom/34_77_e/historic.pdf.

48. French rail system.

49. Congrès Mondial de la Documentation Universelle (World Congress of Universal Documentation), Paris, 1937. At the time, part of the Exposition Internationale des Arts et Techniques.

50. Law governing every association in France.

51. No beginning quote marks are indicated in Briet's original text.

52. Jesse H. Shera (1903–1982). American librarian and library theoretician.

53. These three terms are in English in the original.
54. (1902–1981). Director of the Library of Congress (1945–1954).
55. Institut International de Bibliographie.
56. Jaime Torres-Bodet (1902–1974). Director of UNESCO (1948–1952).
57. In 1950, a group of Danish students came to Valognes library, which is famous for its books dating from the Middle Ages, and which had been damaged in the last year of World War II. On a UNESCO mission, they helped recreate the library catalog.
58. International Council of Museums (UNESCO).
59. Paul Perrier (1886–1965). Colleague of Briet's at the Bibliothèque Nationale, author of *L'Unité Humaine, Histoire de la Civilisation et de l'Esprit Humain* [Human Unity, History of Civilization and of Human Spirit] (Paris: F. Alcan, 1931) and of *L'Unification Humaine* [Human Unification] (Paris, Albin Michel, 1948).
60. The French social and political review *La Revue des Deux Mondes*.
61. The French original is unclear in this sentence: "En effet, plus les masses innombrables et incultes venues de tous les champs de la liberté sont appelées à monter en ligne, plus il est nécessaire de les instruire, de les éclairer, de les assister culturellement."
62. "Quel siècle à mains!" Arthur Rimbaud, *Une Saison en Enfer*. "J'ai horreur de tous les métiers. Maîtres et ouvriers, tous paysans, ignobles. La main à plume vaut la main à charrue. —Quel siècle à mains !—"

~

"A Necessity of Our Time": Documentation as "Cultural Technique" in *What Is Documentation?*

Ronald E. Day

The "Cultural or Functional Specialization" of Documentation

Suzanne Briet's small book, *Qu'est-ce que la documentation?* (*What Is Documentation?*), is not only of historical interest, but also of theoretical interest. My own background is neither that of a historian, per se, nor that of a biographer. For a biographical introduction to Briet, we have included in this volume Michael Buckland's brief biography. For a history of French documentation and its European context, the English reader will have to read in French or await a translation of Sylvie Fayet-Scribe's *Histoire de la Documentation en France: Culture, Science et Technologie de l'Information:1895–1937*[1] or a similar work. For a combination biography and documentary history, Mary Niles Maack's article "The Lady and the Antelope: Suzanne Briet's Contribution to the French Documentation Movement"[2] is recommended. In this essay, however, I would like to pull together several theoretical issues from Briet's work, largely concentrating on the notion of "culture," and I will end by discussing the importance of one of Briet's particular understandings of the term "culture" for the future of libraries as a particular type of documentation agency. With this reading I wouldn't claim to exhaust the very admirable complexity and subtlety of Briet's book, which I have indicated in the preface to this volume, but rather I want to simply emphasize a certain reading of her work, focusing upon the meaning of "culture" within it. Such an exploration also involves, however, coming to terms with her understanding of the epistemology of documents, a question which we will first engage.

Michael Buckland's article "What Is a Document?"[3] brought Briet's works to historical and critical consciousness in the library and information science community in its discussion of the first few important pages of Briet's *What Is Documentation?* In this article, Buckland poses the question of what constitutes a "document." Briet's *What Is Documentation?* first suggests, citing the definition of "document" from the French Union of Documentation Organizations (UFOD), that documents can be defined as "all bases of materially fixed knowledge, and capable of being used for consultation, study, and proof." From this beginning, Buckland in his article examines documents from the aspect of their being evidence in any physical form.

In her book, though, Briet immediately "counters" this initial definition of documents as evidence, offering another one that less opposes and more amends the first definition, one which, as she writes, has been suggested by "linguists" and "philosophers": "any concrete or symbolic indexical sign [*indice*], preserved or recorded toward the ends of representing, of reconstituting, or of proving a physical or intellectual phenomenon." In the pages immediately following this statement, Briet provides a range of examples demonstrating how and in what social and discursive contexts documents are indexical signs. Documents are shown to be examples—or "evidence"—of things or larger groupings of things: a star is not a document, but a photograph of a star is; a pebble isn't a document, but a pebble in a mineralogical collection is; a wild animal isn't a document, but an animal in a zoo is. A document is evidence insofar as it is an example. Buckland's emphasis, from Briet's initial definition, of documents being any physical form or format remains in this latter definition, but the notion of evidence is developed and begins with intensional, rather than extensional, reference, and it starts with constellations of reference, rather than the self-announcing "fact."

In *What Is Documentation?*, Briet then develops the notions of "initial," or primary, and "secondary" documents. Initial documents are the initially cataloged thing. Secondary documents are all that follow from this. Briet's privileged example is that of a newly discovered antelope. It is a primary document insofar as it is cataloged as an antelope. From then on, the animal is taken up in various other discourses and activities and, in the words of the philosopher Raymond Bayer, whom Briet quotes, "immediately becomes weighted down under a 'vestment of documents' [*vêture de documents*]." The documentary "fertility" of the original "fact" is, from its discovery through its continuous unfolding in social and cultural spaces, dependent upon these discourses, their differences, and their powers for its initial and secondary identities. We may call the primary system of discourse that cultural field which first defines the object as some type of object or initial or primary document (zoology is the field in the case of Briet's antelope), and we may call the secondary system of discourse those cultural fields which make use of an initial cataloging or classification. These secondary systems, for Briet, cover a wide variety of scholarly and popular arenas.

For example, as Briet shows, there are the documentary systems of the popular media, of the cinema, of the academic lecture hall, and many others. These "documentary systems" are, at least in some cases, what we would now call in some disciplines "discursive systems." However, the common documentary element of these discourses and their accompanying social networks is that of naming objects according to institutionally or socially normative systems. In cataloging, objects are placed in relation to other objects based on shared and essential properties and, so, the objects are named accordingly. In formal systems, such as library catalogues, indexes, and so on, these names are composed out of formal classes. The relation of the catalogued name to the object is descriptive within classes. In brief, the naming of an object within Briet's notion of *indice* has a double indexical relationship: the name points to the object and the name reflects the networks in which the object first appears as a named thing, that is, as an example of something (for example, as an example of a new type within the class "antelope").

Surely, given the time and place of Briet's writing (Paris, probably slightly before 1951) and given the epistemology of documents presented, we may suggest that structuralism and semiotics were the "philosophy" and "linguistics" that Briet writes led her to a definition of documents as *indice*. With this latter definition the earlier definition of documents given in the book is not left behind, but rather, it is developed away from a positivist understanding. For Briet, "facts" are rich in meaning through their appearance in multiple forms and series of documents.

As I have pointed out elsewhere,[4] such an extensive network model of scientific and documentary production, such as Briet's text suggests, would not be conceived again until Actor Network Theory nearly 50 years after the publication of *What Is Documentation?* As I noted, the rhetorical similarity between Briet's narrative of the discovery of an antelope and its portrayal in various discursive structures, and Latour's account of the capture and representation of exotic fauna in one of his texts,[5] is striking. We may suppose that Briet's development of a type of network analysis based on the indexical nature of signs and collections of signs originated not only from her familiarity with the "philosophy" and "linguistics" of her day, but also from her background in librarianship and documentation, which involved the practical understanding of naming in library and documentary cataloging and classification systems in relation to specific cultures of scientific and professional practices.

In *What Is Documentation?* Briet's theoretical differences with earlier documentation and with librarianship are clearly presented. The most cutting of Briet's observations in *What Is Documentation?* must be in regard to the dream and the attempt of the father of European Documentation, Paul Otlet, to assemble a universal bibliography. Both praising Otlet's leadership in international bibliography and also marking a substantial break between what we might see as Otlet's first generation documentation and Briet's second generation documentation, Briet writes:

> Little by little, the theory of documentation has grown since the great period of the typographical explosion that began in the third quarter of the nineteenth century, which corresponds to the development of the historical sciences as the progress of technique. OTLET had been its magus, the international leader, with his Institute of Bibliography in Brussels, his universal decimal classification system, his Council of Scientific Unions, and his Mundaneum. Others, less ambitious—or, more prudent—plowed the furrows of a culture that failed, in Otlet's circle, to descend from the clouds. *Documentology* lost nothing in alleviating itself of a Universal Bibliographic Catalog [Répertoire Bibliographique Universel—RBU], which everyone had considered a dream and which did not offer a comparable attraction to the most localized of union catalogues.

For Otlet, documentation would be successful insofar as it provided a universal bibliography, centralized in a world library in a world city. From this storehouse of knowledge, users could be served, one day using television screens to deliver the information to the user who could view it from his or her workstation or armchair.[6] Briet, however, rejects this model as idealistic. The reason for her rejection is central and is illustrated not only in the first few pages, but throughout her book. For Briet there is no need for a centralized universal bibliography; a universal bibliography is better served by a network model of multiple documentary organizations or agencies. Through standardized training (Briet helped found the National Institute of Documentary Techniques [l'Institut National des Techniques de la Documentation (INTD)], which is still part of the National Conservatory of Arts and Crafts [Conservatoire National des Arts et Métiers—the Parisian technical university]), universal bibliography could be achieved much more efficiently than with a bibliographical center. Local agencies of documentation must serve their user population not only by warehousing documents but also by "prospecting" the boundaries of known fields. The documentalist must not only be the "milkmaid" of science, retrieving new documents for the scholar, but as Briet puts it elsewhere, documentalists must be like the "dog on the hunt, in advance of the researcher, guided, guiding."[7] This role of not only professional service but also expert prospecting, within and at the edges of a given "cultural field" of science, is an important attribute that we will soon return to.

Briet's break with Otlet's vision of documentation occurs not only in regard to the centralization of bibliography and the "cultural" expertise of the documentalist but also in regard to the role of the documentalist in relation to the users of documentary services. This is where the user emphasis of the American library tradition, and in particular, the special library tradition, comes into conflict with the European library tradition stressing collection building and closed stacks. Briet, as we may recall, was the founder of the Salle des Catalogues et Bibliographies—the reference room—at the Bibliothèque Nationale. For Briet, the documentalist must locate him- or herself intellectually, and even institutionally, beside the researcher. The reasons for this are several. First, there is the need for expertise in the technical or academic field in which the documentalist works (this is an important part of what Briet means when she stresses that documentation must have a cultural specialization). Second, there is the need for the documentalist to find new materials at the cutting edge of research in the field and as the field overlaps with other fields. Third is the importance that Briet places upon documentation as part of scientific research. Since prospecting for information is part of the documentalist's job, Briet views the documentalist as integral to discovery and communication in science and in scholarship as a whole.

This division between the first (Otlet) and the second (Briet) generation of documentation runs parallel to the difference between librarianship and documentation that Briet marks in *What Is Documentation?* The difference here is that documentation is involved not simply with subject specialization, particularly in regard to the privileged form of the book; instead, documentation is a "*cultural*" specialization from which the material and aesthetic form of the document issues. For Briet, the "human sciences" (and with them, libraries) are largely concerned with the value of accumulated materials. The traditional form of this accumulation is the entity of the book. The sciences, on the other hand, are "revolutionary." For Briet, the sciences function by advancing or overturning past work, and so they neither are limited to nor do they privilege books, and with them, libraries. Whereas "the book" for Otlet was the privileged material object, as well as a trope that stood for all forms of documentation, the practice of documentation, and the whole of human knowledge, for Briet, the book is largely a relic of an earlier type of scholarship that lingers in the human sciences, and its form has since become dispersed in other documentary forms more suited to more networked and "revolutionary" types of intellectual production. The documentation agency sees books as but one—a historically specific and important, but isolated—form of document.

Since Briet sees prospecting and the documentary diffusion of materials as central to the documentalist's work, the documentalist, claims Briet, has both a central role and a creative role in the development of knowledge across "multi-formed documents." This claim marks a strong difference with the traditional library task of building collections of largely paper-based and bound materials. The gravitational center of libraries is books and book collections, and the central orientation of librarians, even today, is toward these forms. The gravitational center of documentation centers is the social or professional network that is serviced and the various types of materials of any physical type or form that may be used therein. Whereas the library ethos precludes performing scholarly work for the scholar, Briet argues that documentalists may be involved with reading and abstracting materials for the scholars they serve as well as with the "creative" tasks of juxtaposing and likewise arranging materials to produce new insights. The documentalist is focused upon the "cultural" or "functional" networks (inclusive of discourses) and tasks of a specialization. This, what Briet terms cultural "orientation," or what we may call "attunement," is central for the documentalist profession:

> Thus, we now perceive two tendencies: with librarians, the concern is that of producing card catalogs, and consequently increasingly vast, almost universal union catalogs which are able to respond to the question: where can one find a particular work, a rare edition?—without respect to the subject involved. On the other side, with documentalists, there is an effort to prospect and divulge the very diverse means of access to multi-form documents, with the means specific to each discipline. These two tendencies correspond to the specialty of the professions: the former is essentially related to the form of documents, the latter is centered on the cultural or functional specialization. The researchers and scholars find their rewards in these two enterprises of current awareness and orientation.

"A New Cultural Technique"

Given this "cultural or functional specialization" within a practice, Briet's concept of the "cultural necessity" of documentation might, however, also be read as having a grander, more historical, referent than that of specific sets of practices and discourses in science or scholarship: "Culture," with a capital "C," as we might write. There is some evidence of this in her writing. Here, one must closely examine the rhetorical structure of her texts that marks a particular form of historicity, that of progress and development: "efficiency," "dynamism," "inevitability," "necessity," "our time." For example, Briet states in her article, "Bibliothécaires et documentalistes":

> It is necessary to return to [Robert] Pagès. His message has not had, at the moment or when he made his statements, all the discussion that is merited, because it lacked an audience prepared to receive it. This is why, two years later [in *What Is Documentation?*], we attempted to explain those things, which, in our eyes, were documentation: a technique of intellectual work, a new profession, a need of our *time*. Pagès' dialectics and axioms are irrefutable. They may be summarized through some phrases pulled from his text and placed end to end: the crisis of definition which we suffer from is only a symptom of an organizational crisis and a division of cultural work; an inevitable industrialization of intellectual work has produced the machinery (organizations and tools) that make the evolution of a new cultural technique necessary, a technique which will soon be socially decisive. Documentation is a segment of culture, but it includes the domain of librarians: the librarian is a particular case of the documentalist—both are distributors of culture. The duties of the librarian, in fact, aren't fulfilled until she learns general documentary technique.[8]

"Homo documentator," Briet states in the beginning of the second chapter of *What Is Documentation?* is "born out of new conditions of research and of technology (*technique*)." Here, the French word *technique* could just as well be translated with both the English words "technology" and "technique." Throughout *Qu'est-ce que la documentation?* there exists for the English reader an ambiguity in the French word *technique*. The word can mean the equivalent of either "technique" or "technology." The cultural conditions that Briet sees documentation being born within are those of industrial modernity and its means of production through techniques, tools, and various combinations of these. For Briet, technique and technology—production by means of "the brain" and "the hand"—run parallel to one another and converge in modern production:

> The moment has arrived to prove that the exercise of documentation, with all its possibilities and all of its perfected means effectively constitutes a *new cultural technique*. Documentation is becoming more and more technical, as a specialized skill. M. Le ROLLAND has told us that the hand provides for thought,

just as a task that is partly manual serves culture, that is to say, it enriches man. He cites Julian HUXLEY: "The hands receive a precise tactile image from the materials they handle, the eyes receive a precise image from what they see. . . . The most complete definition of objects by conceptual thought has been followed by their most complete mastery by means of tools and machines." The hand has served the mind; the tool has developed the brain. The brain in turn guides the hand. Such is the omnipresence of intelligence. "Documentation is to culture as the machine is to industry" (PAGÈS).

The blending of technology and technique and intellectual and mechanical tools in documentation leads Briet to praise the work being done at MIT in cybernetics:

The progress of cybernetics, especially at the Massachusetts Institute of Technology, links the complicated precision of an already old automatism to the flashy quickness of more effective electro-technical applications. The documentalist will be more and more dependent upon tools whose technicality increases with great rapidity.

But beyond the technical/technological character of documentation, there are other cultural elements that make it "a necessity for our time." Briet's book clearly spells these out: it is documentation's "dynamism" and "efficiency" that give to it a certain "rhythm." This rhythm is a sympathetic response to the more general information and communication technologies that have affected scholarship and which documentation, too, incorporates within itself:

Still, the tools of intellectual work have deeply transformed the attitude of the scholar, whatever his specialty may be. The factors of space and time intervene much more than in the past. The hourly calendar, the telephone, the microfilm reader, the typewriter, the Dictaphone, and the teletype give to intellectual work a *different rhythm*.

This observation may be Briet's most important, at least in terms of cultural theory, and it underpins her book's attempt to argue that documentation is not *just* a "cultural technique" (in terms of its fitting into particular cultural modes of production), but that it is an *exemplary* and *necessary* technique of cultural modernity as a whole. Information and communication technologies may introduce a "new rhythm" to society and culture, but they themselves are a "symptom" of Western social development. Technique and technology are, thus, two historically specific social and cultural symptoms to which documentation responds, not only by incorporating them, but also by incorporating Western modernity's opposite trend toward global expansion. Thus, the double "rhythm" of documentation tends toward both analytical specialization and global expansion. Since Briet's task is not to question, but to "adapt" and, indeed, to grasp and control this new rhythm through documentary techniques and technology, she doesn't seem to see the cultural and social narrowness of this orientation toward simultaneous specialization and global expansion. Specifically, the "new humanism" she speaks of seems very much that of *a* culture, namely, what she sometimes identifies as the Western "modern":

> It is not too much to speak of a new *humanism* in this regard. A different breed of researchers "is in the making." It springs from the reconciliation of the machine and the mind. Modern man cannot repudiate any aspect of his heritage. Relying on the rich experiences of the past that have been passed on to him, he resolutely turns toward the world of tomorrow. The constant development of humanity requires that the masses and the individual adapt. Here, technology [*technique*] is the symptom of a social need. "One characteristic of modern documentation is that of the coordination" of diverse "sectors in the same organization."
>
> Thus, documentation appears as the *corrective* to ever advancing *specialization*. Closed within the more or less spacious limits of his specialty, the researcher needs to be guided through the frontier regions of his particular domain. Orientation along the margins of a subject, prospecting some of the sources in an area of research, determining expertise—these are the many requirements involved in the coordination of diverse activities.

Techniques and technologies are expressions of culture for Briet, and this "heritage" of culture, according to Briet, cannot be refused. In terms of scholarly writing and publishing and in terms of documentary production and use, Briet saw her culture undergoing a radical historical change. The change was from a medieval and early modern manner for the composition and production of knowledge, based on personal understanding, small personal libraries, and, later, books and book distribution to a modern scientific manner of knowledge production, based on cultural, social, and documentary networks for knowledge production and multiple documentary forms for its embodiment and distribution. The medieval *intellectus* (the universe as contemplated by the intellect, substantiated in, and signified as "the book") is replaced by multiple authorship and the social accumulation of knowledge; the book as the container and the trope for knowledge (Otlet) is replaced by networks of multiple documentary-form objects. Equally, this new emphasis upon networks of knowledge rather than a centralized "book" or site of knowledge means a new importance given to "bibliography" (using the "pre-documentalist" term) as not only a documentary event but also a cultural and social event. The essence of networks as cultural grounds lie in the "references" that run through them, as their rhizomic "roots." In the mode of documentation, even libraries are seen to rest on these rhizomic roots of "references":

> During the reorganization of the internal services and stacks of the Biblio-thèque National [sic], Paris, in 1934, a separate place was found for the Cata-logues and Bibliographies Room: —it was installed in the basement. Subter-ranean, cryptic, with its roots running in every direction through the substructure of knowledge, bibliography can be fairly said to fit into the foun-dation of library science. Without it there can be no scholarly research, no pos-itive identifications, no enlightened acquisitions, no guides to reading. It is, at the same time, the source and nourishment of the intellectual life of our time. Napoleon once said something like this, "Give me your references and I can do without your report."[9]

In Briet's modernity—the modernity of "documentation"—knowledge is explicitly *embedded* and *emergent* in cultural and social production. The doc-umentalist is located in specialized centers, working with, but also in a sense, ahead of, the scientist or scholar. Documentation doesn't serve personal un-derstanding as we sit in our armchairs in each of our own personal studies, but instead, documentation is part of public spaces of production—social networks and cultural forms. Knowledge, for Briet, is primarily social and cul-tural, and the production of documents is part of the social and cultural pro-duction of knowledge. Briet's lengthy description at the beginning of her book of all the networks through which the newly discovered antelope is em-bodied suggests both the constituting power of social-discursive networks and cultural forms in giving value to an object and the power of the object to shuttle across discursive boundaries and to create relationships—quite liter-ally, worlds—where none existed previously:

> In our age of multiple and accelerated broadcasts, the least event, scientific or political, once it has been brought into public knowledge immediately be-comes weighted down under a "vestment of documents" (Raymond Bayer). Let us admire the documentary fertility of a simple originary fact: for example, an antelope of a new kind has been encountered in Africa by an explorer who has succeeded in capturing an individual that is then brought back to Europe for our Botanical Garden [Jardin des Plantes]. A press release makes the event

known by newspaper, by radio, and by newsreels. The discovery becomes the topic of an announcement at the Academy of Sciences. A professor of the Museum discusses it in his courses. The living animal is placed in a cage and cataloged (zoological garden). Once it is dead, it will be stuffed and preserved (in the Museum). It is loaned to an Exposition. It is played on a soundtrack at the cinema. Its voice is recorded on a disk. The first monograph serves to establish part of a treatise with plates, then a special encyclopedia (zoological), then a general encyclopedia. The works are cataloged in a library, after having been announced at publication (publisher catalogues and Bibliography of France). The documents are recopied (drawings, watercolors, paintings, statues, photos, films, microfilms), then selected, analyzed, described, translated (documentary productions). The documents that relate to this event are the object of a scientific classifying (fauna) and of an ideologic [*idéologique*] classifying (classification). Their ultimate conservation and utilization are determined by some general techniques and by methods that apply to all documents—methods that are studied in national associations and at international Congresses.

Modernity, for Briet, involves the growth of networks of knowledge within the progress of "civilization." Thus, as Briet states in the conclusion to her book, documentation is an essential mechanism of the "growing society" that she sees as a fact around her, one that spreads to the colonies and the "hinterlands." Quoting Paul Perrier, the ideals of Enlightenment Europe, particularly after the Second World War—"universal suffrage, compulsory schooling, the battle against epidemics, the progress of feminism, social laws, the organization of work, constitutions and political parties," spread through both "imitation" as well as "economic necessity." The world grows toward unity, following the global diffusion and establishment of ideals, values, associations, and materials.

For Briet, documentation is part of the spread and diffusion of "science" and Western modernity, in general. For Briet, what she sees as "science" and "development" are worldwide cultural events that are brought to postcolonial countries, following in the wake of "the United Nations flag." The following needs to be quoted in full, for it is a powerful rhetorical passage that demonstrates the historical, social, and cultural destiny that Briet sees in documentation:

Since the Second World War, *UNESCO* has played the chief role in assembling and energizing experts and organizations in the educational and cultural field. Its Division of Libraries, under the direction of Edw. CARTER, has systematically pursued, in relation to other sections of UNESCO, a cultural policy that guarantees that its current results will be passed onto the future. "The living republic of minds" (J. TORRES-BODET) is being created through a subterranean evolution with the United Nations as the temporary perhaps, but useful, frame. Some outposts of scientific cooperation (Manila, Delhi, Cairo, Montevideo) are points of departure for missionaries of a new type, charged with the cultural development of the more or less uncultured masses and with multiplying contacts with scholars. The technical assistants of UNESCO, in fact, have available a sometimes immense "hinterland" to explore and organize. It is through reciprocal actions and reactions that these outposts spread out and are scientifically informed. The battle against illiteracy, the organization of a reading public, of librarianship, and of documentation in all its forms, comes in the wake of this exploration vessel flying the United Nations flag.

The "cultural technique" of documentation issues both from particular occupational cultures in Western modernity and from Western modernity as a whole. To our eyes, today, Briet's faith in the inevitable and necessary spread of Western modern science and knowledge may be perplexing. Equally striking, in a different manner though, is the difference between Briet's vision of documentation's globalism and that of Otlet's. Otlet saw all the cultures of the world centrally assembled—bibliographically, diplomatically, educationally—in European institutions and cities. European soil and the European Enlightenment would be the literal and intellectual grounds for world culture. Briet's vision of globalism is, however, that of postwar Western internationalism and "development": the necessary and active diffusion of Western ideals into other cultural, social, and geographical spaces. For Briet, Western scientific and Enlightenment values are the seeds through which the world as a whole grows together.

Cultures and the Collapse of the Meaning of "Culture"

One area where differences in culture can be immediately grasped, particularly in a documentary domain, is that of language. For Briet, on the one hand, linguistic multiplicity allows a work to be read in multiple languages. On the other, however, the "Babel" of languages hinders the diffusion of documents and ideas. Whereas Otlet and other internationalists of his generation took hope in an artificially created language (Esperanto) in order to mediate global linguistic Babel, Briet's internationalist vision, instead, poses three privileged languages (English, French, and Spanish) as documentary intermediaries to other languages. Here, once again, we can view Briet's understanding of documentation against that of Otlet's: for Briet, documentation is founded on key institutions and standards as routes for connecting cultures (in the senses of both organizational and national cultures). In the ideology of postwar development, European culture provided these standards and its history of Western colonialism provided their conduits. However, by sort of a reverse capture, so too, the words, concepts, attitudes, and other cultural materials of "the West" are appropriated by its "others," not only outside, but also within, the geographical boundaries of what we think of as Europe and the Americas. Though Briet's book doesn't explicitly mark this reverse appropriation, its valorization of local cultures as originary sites for documentary meaning and production logically lead to this concept.

The extension of Western modernity—in a sense, the overextension and "implosion" of the meaning of "culture" in the West—may be seen as the limit to Briet's use of the term "culture" in the grander sense, that is, Western "Culture" with a capital "C." Briet depends upon the notion of Western modernist Culture in not only arguing for the "necessity" but also implying the historical inevitability of documentation. But what would happen to documentation if the notion of "culture," in the sense of "localized" or specialized cultures, were extended to the point that there was no Culture, per se, that one could point to as being the former sense's guiding and determining historical spirit? Analogously, one could ask today, which "English" is now spoken worldwide? What is the meaning of "democracy?" Is there *a* culture in Europe or North America today? Can we speak of "the West" in either a determined historical, geographical, or cultural sense, or must we see "the West," and along with it, "culture" (in both the larger and smaller senses of the word) as social networks and expressive affordances? Indeed, the practical service of documentation to *cultures* seems to promote the collapse of the concept of "Culture" as a concept upon which to dream the harmony of a single world, not to mention "Culture" as a historical spirit that determines the inevitability of documentation itself. And yet, in Briet's time and work, and as we have suggested, in a different way in Otlet's earlier time and work, the dream of world harmony was the very goal of documentation:

> It has become commonplace, however, to affirm that humanity strives toward *unity*. The historical sketch that Paul PERRIER has given of this evolution over the centuries is striking. He insists on the ineluctability of the law of unification that he has discovered in his patient, historical work. He explains the success and failure of regressive or progressive human enterprises. He has put into perspective the role of international relations in our time . . . .

With this collapse of *Culture* by *cultures*, we are left with a question: what is the meaning of documentation without *Culture*? Where does documentation issue from if not from Culture? One may be reminded here of Walter Benjamin's description of Baudelaire, imaginatively stabbing into the crowd with his pen in order to control the chaos into which the unique individual, as the basis for lyric poetry, had fallen, only to have "the crowd" send his lyrical self into the streets. If Benjamin was correct, that an older form of expression adjusts to new social rhythms that put inexorable pressures upon it by attempting to duplicate the opposing social rhythms in its own expressions, so today, in documentation, we now see an expansion of documentary forms far beyond writing, the explosion of scholarly fields into other fields (so much so that the notion of "fields" becomes problematic) and cultural fusions of many types. "Documentation" seems now to be less an expression of Western (modernist) Culture, less to be characterized by the tropes that were supposed to represent that culture (foremost in modernism, efficiency, and dynamism) and now to be more constituted by material necessity. It is material necessity that seems, today, to constitute the call of documentation, not Culture or at least, not any one culture. And where that material necessity leads, and what documentation expresses of it, will very much vary depending upon the people who use "documents." "Culture," in this sense, is not a unifying term (as in Otlet), nor is it a historical *Geist* or *Esprit*, and there is no particular "development" which documentation can ride in the wake of and claim as the origin of its own historical necessity. Rather, "cultures" may be seen in the expressions of various documents and documentary practices. This "open," "cultural" reading of "culture," as well as documentation, is the one that Briet's book suggests, even as it allies itself with the legacy of a historicist reading of "culture," seemingly for professional reasons.

The culture of documentation, as "a necessity of our time," is that of documentary *cultures* operating within, and as a product of, various types of other cultures, specific cultures that the documentalist must be familiar with and prospect at the edge of. Cultures give us whatever we may call, subsequently, "documents" and from this, documentalists. In this, Briet demonstrates herself an interesting theorist, not only of the library and the documentary professions, but also as a cultural theorist at large. Documentation is, for Briet, the way forward for "culture" but it is the way forward that will dissolve "culture" as a unifying term, at least in regard to what we call, "the West." Information and communication technologies and techniques are privileged in Briet's work as a force that collapses Culture into cultures, allowing the many cultures to disseminate and dissolve the metaphysical entity of "the West." What remains of "modernity" is precisely what Briet most emphasizes: technologies and techniques, now appropriated by those "other" cultures for whom "the West" remains somewhat more material than the term "culture" suggests, and more pressing than a narrative of transcendental historical "necessity" allows. Such a vision stood opposed to Otlet's centralizing model, and it still stands opposed to some visions of the global future.

"Culture" and the Future of Libraries

Needless to add, "libraries" are often seen as the seat or heart of "culture." Libraries, as we know them today, are very specific to modernism, particularly to nineteenth-century modernism. Briet's vision of documentation as encompassing, but historically advancing beyond libraries and librarianship, points to the dispersal or dissolution of physical libraries, just as it points to the dissolution of Culture. The dispersal of the concept of the modern library and the dissolution of its physical presence is seen in our own time in the shift to digital libraries, which are beginning to follow the very decentralized model for collection and service that Briet's understandings of documentation centers and agencies and the roles of the documentalist point to. The term "bibliography" now covers the notion of citation across the entire Internet and across physical forms different from books. "Reference"—in its various meanings—constitutes part of bibliography, but also involves social networks, just as Briet suggested by her grounding of documentation in social networks and cultural forms. Indeed, Briet's understanding of documentation points to the end of libraries as we have known them as cornerstones or "centers" of Culture and toward "libraries"—in whatever institutional or noninstitutional form this term may be imagined in the present and future—as techniques and technologies of linkage between documents within "cultures." Briet's book seems to say, "Do you understand? Here is the future: libraries are no longer the center of documentation, but instead, we must now concentrate on techniques and technologies of documentation serving and being used by specific cultures across a broad range of documentary forms, social networks, and cultural means of expression. These will be our new 'libraries.'" Briet's "documentation centers" are, after all, founded through cultural productions, not before them. Instead of libraries as the cornerstone *of* Culture, documentation centers and other agencies embody particular techniques and technologies as services of and to *cultures*. The material form and the privileged trope of "the book" have been surpassed in numbers and kind by the document, of which the book is only one kind among a nonclosed set of kinds. There is no end to the physical forms or formats of documents since documents are products of cultures and, thus, there is no end to types of documentary centers and the techniques and technologies that they employ. The term "library" no longer simply refers to a physical space that concentrates on the collection and lending of books, but now the term refers more generally to collections of data or documents of any type, organized to serve cultures of users.

Thus, Briet's *What Is Documentation?* remains a "necessity of our time" in that it points to the possibilities and limits of "culture" and with that, the possibilities and limits of any professional practice that seeks to justify itself on "cultural" grounds. On the one hand, the book marked the height of Culture (as Otlet proclaimed), and particularly what has been called "the culture of the book." On the other hand, Briet's understanding of documentation marks the importance of particular, more "localized" or specialized cultures in terms of their material needs, their specialized vocabularies, and the techniques and technologies needed to provide documentary services to these groups. It isn't that books will disappear, but rather, that books, and with them, libraries as the temple of books, are becoming specific cultural items, rather than an exemplar of Culture. These transformations will take some time, but they are already occurring and are inevitable. Cultural groups use and demand a potentially infinite array of types and forms of what may be called "documents." Thus, the notion of a "library" is expanded to such a degree that its modern cultural-institutional meaning becomes historically bracketed and historically specific, and its power is dispersed over a wider space. Just as Culture is transformed in cultures, so the Library is dispersed into documentary techniques and technologies. This is something that still needs to be seen and reckoned with in library education and in library institutions. Briet wrote of it a half century ago, and these changes have only increased since then.

Notes

1. Sylvie Fayet-Scribe, *Histoire de la documentation en France: culture, science et technologie de l'information: 1895–1937* (Paris: CNRS Éditions, 2000).

2. Mary Niles Maack, "The Lady and the Antelope: Suzanne Briet's Contribution to the French Documentation Movement," *Library Trends* 53 (Spring 2004): 719–47.

3. Michael K. Buckland, "What Is a Document?" *Journal of the American Society of Information Science* 48, no. 9 (Sept. 1997): 804–9.

4. Ronald E. Day, *The Modern Invention of Information: Discourse, History, and Power* (Carbondale: University of Illinois Press, 2001).

5. Bruno Latour, "Ces réseaux que la raison ignore: laboratoires, bibliothèques, collections," *Le Pouvoir des Bibliothèques: la Mémoire des Livres en Occident* (Paris: Albin Michel, 1996), 23–46.

6. Paul Otlet, *Monde: Essai d'Universalisme: Connaissance du Monde, Sentiment du Monde, Action Organisée et Plan du Monde* (Brussels: Editiones Mundaneum, 1935).

7. Suzanne Briet, "Bibliothécaires et documentalistes," *Revue de la Documentation* 21 (1954): 43.

8. Suzanne Briet, "Bibliothécaires et documentalistes," *Revue de la Documentation* 21 (1954): 44.

9. Suzanne Briet, "Bibliography in the Basement," *Special Libraries*, February 1950: 52. I am grateful to Michael Buckland for finding this source and for pointing out this passage.

~

Writings by Suzanne Renée Briet:
A Selective Bibliography

Compiled by Michael K. Buckland

Items are listed by year within two sections: (1) Documentation and Librarianship and (2) History, Literature, and Other Topics. Note Briet's occasional use of the names S. Dupuy, S. Dupuy-Briet, and S. Briet-Dupuy.

For a more complete listing, see Michael Buckland, "Suzanne Renée Briet 1894–1989: Checklist of Writings," URL: www.sims.berkeley.edu/~buckland/Brietwebbib.pdf.

1. Documentation and Librarianship

S. Dupuy, "L'activité bibliographique et documentaire à la Bibliothèque nationale (et liste générale des catalogues)," *Revue des bibliothèques* 42e année, 1 & 2 trimestres, t. 39 (1932): 5–49. "Liste des catalogues utiles de la Bibliothèque nationale" is found on pages 21–49.

"Le Centre national d'information bibliographique (Rome)," *Revue des bibliothèques* 43–44 années, t. 40 (1933–1934): 252–55. Translation by S. Dupuy of most of "Il Centro nazionale di informazioni bibliografiche," *Accademie e Biblioteche d'Italia* 5, no. 3–4 (feb. 1932): 296–98.

"La terminologie des sciences de la documentation," in International Institute for Documentation, 9th conference, 1932. *Rapports* (Brussels: I.I.D.) 101–7. Also in *La documentation en France* (mai 1932): 1–12.

S. Dupuy-Briet. "Le Congrès de bibliographie et de documentation (1932)," *Revue des bibliothèques* 42e année—1932, 39, no. 4 (1932): [392]–394. International Institute for Documentation, 11th conference, 1932, Frankfurt am Main.

S. Dupuy-Briet, "Le Bureau de renseignements allemand et la bibliographie officielle en France," *Revue des bibliothèques* 43–44 années, t. 40 (1933–1934): [401]–417. Report to the Minister of Education on the Auskunftsbureau at the Preussische Staatsbibliothek.

"De nouveau à la Bibliothèque nationale," *Bulletin du bibliophile et du bibliothécaire* N.S., 13e année (20 mai 1934): 210–13.

S. Dupuy. [Entwurf einer Terminologie für Dokumentation] in International Institute for Documentation, 12th conference, 1933. *Rapports*. I.I.D. Publ. 172a. (Brussels: I.I.D., 1934), 9.

"La nouvelle salle des catalogues à la Bibliothèque nationale," *Revue du Livre 2*, no. 7 (1934): 170–75.

La Documentation en France: Répertoire des centres de documentation existant en France (Paris: Union française des organismes de documentation, 1935). Compiled by S. Briet.

"Les services bibliographiques à la bibliothèque de Vienne," *Revue des bibliothèques* 45e–46e années, 1935–36, t. 41, no. 1 (1935–1936): 82–83.

"La science chimique et les livres; une visite à la Maison de la chimie," *Archives et bibliothèques 2* (1936): 158–61.

"La documentation au service des techniques," *Bulletin du bibliophile et du bibliothécaire* N.S., 16e année (20 octobre 1937): 246–53.

"La documentation en France; esquisse de l'effort français pour la documentation universelle," in World Congress of Universal Documentation, 1937. *Communications* (Paris: Secrétariat [of Congress]), 49–51.

"Le premier congrès mondial de la documentation," *Bulletin du bibliophile et du bibliothécaire* N.S., 16e année (20 octobre 1937): 437–46.

"Le 'Bulletin de documentation bibliographique'; historique, description, utilité," in International Federation for Documentation, 14th conference, 1938, Oxford and London. *Rapports*. (The Hague: F.I.D.), C200–C203. About Bulletin issued by the Bibliothèque nationale.

"La nouvelle Salle des catalogues à la Bibliothèque nationale," *Bulletin du bibliophile et du bibliothécaire* N.S., 17e année (20 octobre 1938): 437–42.

"La documentation à la Bibliothèque nationale de Paris," *F.I.D. Communications 9*, fasc. 4 (1943), 49–51.

Association Française de Normalisation. Direction des Bibliothèques. *Code de catalogage des imprimés communs. Dictionnaire des cas*. Mme Briet, Mme A. Puget-Payen: rédactrices (Paris: AFB, 1945).

Review by T. Besterman, *Journal of Documentation 1* (1945): 165–66.

"La documentation en France, 1940–5," *Journal of Documentation 1* (1945): 125–35. In French with English summary.

"L'enseignement de la documentation en France," in International Federation for Documentation, 16th conference, Paris, 1946. *Rapports* (The Hague: F.I.D., 1946), vol. 3, C161–64.

"Guide international des organismes de documentation et manuels nationaux de la recherche documentaire." [Followed by "Questionnaire" and "International documentation directory: Preliminary note"] in International Federation for Documentation, 16th conference, Paris, 1946. *Rapports* (The Hague: F.I.D., 1946), vol. 3, C114–20.

Also published in *Revue de la Documentation* 14, no. 2 (1947): 91–97. "L'enseignement de la documentation en France," *Revue de la Documentation* 14, no. 1 (1947): 30–33. Describes the two-year course of training at the Institut National des Techniques de la Documentation.

"La terminologie et les règles bibliographiques à la commission des analyses de l'UNESCO, Paris 20–25 juin 1949," *Revue de la Documentation* 16, no. 4 (1949): 100–101. Recommendations forwarded to ISO-TC46.

Abstract: *Journal of Documentation* 5, no. 3 (Dec. 1949): 189.

"Formation professionelle des bibliothécaires et documentalistes. *Revue de la Documentation* 16, Fasc. 4 (1949): 106–13; 17, Fasc. 1 (1950): 18–19; and 18, Fasc. 1 (1951): 21–27.

Brief summaries in *Journal of Documentation* 5, no. 3 (1949) and *Journal of Documentation* 6, no. 1 (1950): 50.

"Bibliography in the Basement," *Special Libraries* 41 (1950): 52–55. About bibliographies at the Bibliothèque nationale.

"La documentation en France de 1945 à 1950," *ABCD: Archives, Bibliothèques, Collections, Documentation* 1 (mai–juin 1951): 2–27.

Enquiry Concerning Professional Education of Librarians and Documentalists: Final Report presented to the Joint Committee of the International Federation of Library Associations and of the International Federation for Documentation. (UNESCO/CUA/2). (Paris: UNESCO, 1951). Also published in French in 1950. Summary of reports by 102 specialists in 35 countries.

Reviews by E. A. Jensen, *Libri* 2, no. 4 (1953): 357–78 and by R. Stokes, *Journal of Documentation* 8, no. 3 (Sept. 1952): 178–79.

Qu'est-ce que la documentation? (Paris: ÉDIT, 1951).

Review (1952) by V. W. Clapp, *Library of Congress Information Bulletin* 11 (January 28): 1–3.

Spanish translation: *Que es la documentación?* trans. Beatriz Favaro (Argentina, Santa Fé: Universidad nacional del Litoral. Facultad de ciencias jurídicas y sociales. Departamento del extensión universitaria, 1960).

UNESCO and France, Bibliothèques de France (Direction), *Répertoire des bibliothèques de France: 3, Centres et services de documentation* (Paris: Bibliothèque nationale, 1951). Compiled by Suzanne Briet, with the collaboration of Marie-Ange Boucher Chomel.

"L'enseignement et le statut professionnels des bibliothécaires et des documentalistes: Rapport présenté à la Commission jumelée F.I.D./F.I.A.B. (Copenhague, 1er octobre 1952)," *Revue de la Documentation* 19, fasc. 2 (1952): 21–26.

"Bibliothèques et centres de documentation technique aux États Unis; notes d'un voyage de quatre mois (octobre 1951–février 1952)," *ABCD: Archives, Bibliothèques, Collections, Documentation* 11 (1953): 299–308.

"Bibliothécaires et documentalistes," *Revue de la Documentation* 21, fasc. 2 (1954): 41–45.

English summary: *Journal of Documentation* 11, no. 1 (March 1955): 46.

"La formation professionelle des bibliothécaires aux États Unis," *ABCD: Archives, Bibliothèques, Collections, Documentation* 13 (1954): 337–40.

"Formation des bibliothécaires, plus particulièrement en vue de leur participation à la vie économique et sociale," in International Congress of Libraries and Documentation Centres, 1955, Brussels. [*Proceedings*]. (The Hague: M. Nijhoff, 1955–58), vol. 1: 67–71.

2. History, Literature, and Other Topics

S. Briet-Dupuy, *Chants mimés pour nos enfants, avec indications détaillées pour exécution.* (Turs: Arrault & cie, 1937). Printed music scores.

"L''Areopagitica' de Milton, histoire d'une traduction," *Revue de littérature comparée* 26 (1952): 446–56.

Bibliothèque Nationale, *Arthur Rimbaud. Exposition organisée pour le centième anniversaire de sa naissance* (Paris: Bibliothèque nationale, 1954). Exhibition curated and cataloged by S. Briet.

Rimbaud notre prochain: Généalogie, carte, document hors-texte (Paris: Nouvelle éditions latines, 1956).

Le Maréchal de Schulemberg: Jean III, comte de Montdejeux (1598–1671). Les cahiers d'études ardennais 4 (Mézières: Editions de la Société d'Études Ardennaises, Archives départementales, 1960).

Châteaux des Ardennes, Cahiers Ardennais 17 (Mézières: Société des Ecrivains Ardennais, 1963).

"La Bible dans l'oeuvre de Rimbaud," Avant-siècle 6. *Etudes rimbaldiennes* 1 (1968): 87–129.

Madame Rimbaud, essai de biographie, suivi de la correspondance de Vitalie Rimbaud-Cuif dont treize lettres inedites, Avant-siècle 5. (Paris: Lettres modernes, Minard, 1968).

"'Villette,' le roman de Charlotte Brontë, a-t-il influencé quelques poèmes d'Arthur Rimbaud," *Revue de l'histoire littéraire de la France* 68 (1968): 834–40.

"L'humeur de Rimbaud," Avant-siècle 10. *Etudes rimbaldiennes* 2 (1969): 15–40.

"Lépante et l'éternelle question d'Orient," *Ecrits de Paris* 305 (juillet–août 1971): 65–74.

"La signification de 'Mémoire', poème crucial de Rimbaud," Avant-siècle 12. *Etudes rimbaldiennes* 3 (1972): 35–41.

Entre Aisne et Meuse . . . et au delà, Les cahiers ardennais 22 (Charleville-Mezières: Société des Ecrivains Ardennais, 1976).

Suzanne Briet and Jony Villeneuve, "'La Grive': revue ardennaise d'art et de littérature (150 numéros de 1928 à 1973). Extraits d'anciens numéros. Index," in *Jean-Paul Vaillant et la Grive, une aventure littéraire en Ardenne (1925–1985)* [Présentation, Philippe Vaillant; préface, André Dhôtel]. Les classiques ardennais (Lyon: Manufacture, c1985) 137–83. Cover title: *Jean-Paul Vaillant et la revue la Grive*.

~

About the Editors and Contributors

Hermina G. B. Anghelescu earned her master's in foreign languages and literatures (French and English) from the University of Bucharest (Romania), and her M.L.I.S. and Ph.D. from the Graduate School of Library and Information Science, University of Texas at Austin. From 1979 to 1992, Anghelescu was a librarian at the National Library of Romania. Currently, she is assistant professor in the Library and Information Science Program, Wayne State University, Detroit, Michigan. She is the author of numerous articles on international librarianship and library history, and she is active in international library scholarship.

Michael K. Buckland is codirector of the Electronic Cultural Atlas Initiative and emeritus professor of information management and systems at the University of California, Berkeley. After degrees in history at Oxford and librarianship at Sheffield University, he worked as a librarian in England and in the United States. Past positions include dean of the School of Library and Information Studies at Berkeley and assistant vice president for library plans and policies in the University of California system-wide administration. He has published extensively on library services, information management, and the history of documentation and information science.

Ronald E. Day earned his master's in philosophy and his Ph.D. in comparative literature from the State University of New York at Binghamton, and an additional master's degree in library and information science from the University of California, Berkeley. Currently, he is an assistant visiting professor at the School of Library and Information Science at Indiana University. He is the author of numerous articles on the historical, social, cultural, and political contexts of documentation and information and the author of *The Modern Invention of Information: Discourse, History, and Power* (2001).

Laurent Martinet earned his master's degree in moral and political philosophy at La Sorbonne, Paris, in 1993. He graduated from the Institut National des Techniques Documentaires (INTD), Paris, in 2000. He has since worked on the indexing and content management of databases at *L'Express* magazine, Paris, and he is a translator of English documents into French.